Guide to the Nubian Monuments on Lake Nasser

Guide to the Nubian Monuments on Lake Nasser

Jocelyn Gohary

The American University in Cairo Press

For Said, Karim, and Hany,
and in memory of parents and grandparents

Copyright © 1998 by
The American University in Cairo Press
113 Sharia Kasr el Aini
Cairo, Egypt

Third printing 1999

Dar el Kutub No. 10600/97
ISBN 977 424 462 1

Printed in Egypt

Contents

Acknowledgments

In presenting this guide to the Nubian monuments now accessible to those who take the cruise on Lake Nasser, I wish to express my gratitude to a number of people who have helped me to accomplish this. Special thanks go to my editor, Neil Hewison, whose initial enthusiasm spurred me on, and whose constant encouragement and helpful advice have been invaluable.

I would also like my family and friends in Egypt and abroad to know how much I have appreciated their support and patience.

I am most grateful to the following for providing me with illustrations and information: Judy Allen and Mariano Molero Lazaro, Madrid (Dabod); Fumiaki Konno, Iwate, Japan (Qertassi, Wadi al-Sebua, Dakka, Qasr Ibrim); Gilberto and Sofia Modonesi, Milan (Dendur and al-Lesiya); Dr. Aidan Dodson, University of Bristol; Prof. Kenneth Kitchen, University of Liverpool; Dr. Maarten Raven, Rijksmuseum van Oudheden, Leiden; Prof. Dr. Dietrich Wildung, Ägyptisches Museum, Berlin.

Nubia Past and Present

The ancient land of Nubia consisted of the Nile Valley south of Aswan, bordered by the First Cataract in the north and the Fourth Cataract in the south, an area which is now partly in Egypt and partly in Sudan. In pharaonic times the southern frontier of Egypt was at Aswan, where the First Cataract, a series of rock formations which cut across the bed of the Nile, provided a natural dividing-line.

Although linked in several ways by the Nile, racial origins, and overlapping cultures, the lands and peoples of Egypt and Nubia were also markedly different in various respects, linguistically, topographically, physically, and culturally. Until comparatively recently the ancient Nubians were usually regarded as the proverbial 'poor relations' of the Egyptians, having no centralized administration and imitating many facets of ancient Egyptian religion and art. More detailed excavation and research, much of it undertaken or instigated during the Nubian Rescue Campaign in the 1960s and 1970s, have provided strong evidence for a number of clearly defined phases in Nubian history, with aspects that were peculiar to Nubia, and with indications of African as well as Egyptian influence at certain times. As with its more famous northern neighbor, Nubia went through fluctuations of prosperity and decline, power and anarchy, during its long history, which can be traced back to around 11,000 BC.

The name 'Nubia' is a relatively modern appellation for the region, having first been used by the Greek historian Strabo around 29 BC. It has been suggested that the name is derived

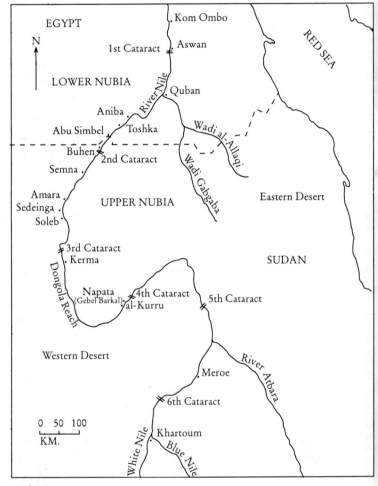

EGYPT

N

.Kom Ombo

1st Cataract ‗. Aswan

RED SEA

LOWER NUBIA

River Nile

.Quban

Aniba .

Abu Simbel .   . Toshka

Wadi al-Allaqi

Buhen ‗
Semna .   2nd Cataract

Wadi Gabgaba

Amara .
Sedeinga .
Soleb ·

UPPER NUBIA

Eastern Desert

‗3rd Cataract
. Kerma

SUDAN

Napata   ‗4th Cataract
(Gebel Barkal) ·al-Kurru

5th Cataract ‗

Dongola Reach

Western Desert

River Atbara

. Meroe

‗6th Cataract

0 50 100
KM.

Khartoum .

White Nile

Blue Nile

Nubia

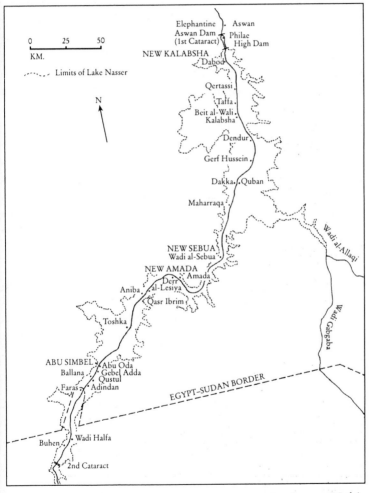

Lower Nubia

from the ancient Egyptian word *nbw* (usually pronounced 'nebu'), meaning 'gold,' a commodity that was extensively mined in the northeastern part of Nubia during the pharaonic and Greco-Roman periods, but there is no proof of this. The ancient Egyptians called it Ta-Sety, the 'Land of the Bow,' referring to the weapon for which the Nubians were famous. The names Yam and Irem were also used at different times, but may have designated particular districts of the country. During the Egyptian New Kingdom (1570–1070 BC), when Nubia was again taken over as a part of Egypt itself, it was divided into two administrative regions, Wawat (Lower Nubia), the area between the First and Second cataracts, and Kush (Upper Nubia), beyond the Second Cataract.

In contrast to the Nile Valley in Egypt, where there was almost invariably an area of cultivated land beside the Nile, Nubia had no continuous stretches of cultivation, but there were pockets of agricultural land, some small, some extensive, separated by large areas of desert with rugged sandstone hills and outcrops. In some places, sand-dunes came right down to the water's edge. On the whole, Lower Nubia, the region with which this book is chiefly concerned, was the more fertile area.

Due to its location between sub-Saharan Africa and Egypt, Nubia acted as an important trading link between Africa and the Mediterranean. Nubia itself provided cattle, manpower, semiprecious stones, gold, and copper, while more exotic items such as ostrich feathers and eggs, ebony, elephant ivory, leopard skins, and incense, came from further south.

The Nubians and the ancient Egyptians were ethnically linked, although the Nubians were darker-skinned and had curlier hair, features that were reflected in the depictions of Nubians in Egyptian art. Their languages were distinct, however, Nubian being a Nilo-Saharan language, while ancient Egyptian was an Afro-Asiatic one. The Nubians were regarded as inferior by the sophisticated Egyptians, particularly during the New Kingdom, when the land south of the First Cataract was frequently described as 'vile Kush,' no doubt referring to the 'uncivilized' inhabitants as well as to the inhospitable nature of the area.

Prehistory (25,000–3500 BC)

By about 25,000 BC both Lower Nubia and Egypt consisted of large areas of savanna land with lush natural vegetation and various forms of wildlife on both sides of the Nile, where nomadic hunter-gatherers found plentiful fish in the river, and wild game such as cattle, gazelle, and antelope on the plains. Sometimes they made seasonal camps beside the river, where they made their stone tools and carved on the rocks around them pictures of the animals they saw and hunted: elephants, giraffes, ostriches, and gazelle.

From 12,000 BC there is evidence of more permanent settlements in both Nubia and southern Upper Egypt, pottery production reflecting this, the earliest instance in Nubia occurring around 6000 BC with the Khartoum Mesolithic culture near modern Khartoum. Over the next two millennia hunting and fishing were gradually supplemented by the domestication of cattle and growing of cereal crops. The situation in Lower Nubia was similar around 4000 BC, where evidence has also been found for settlement and domestication, but the Lower Nubian cultures are more closely connected with the Upper Egyptian culture of the time to the north, rather than the Khartoum culture to the south, and may subsequently have influenced the contemporary Badarian culture in Egypt between 5000 and 4500 BC, as is indicated by the similarity between pottery, tools, and raw materials used by both cultures. Typical of the interchange of culture between Nubia and Egypt is the fact that the succeeding Upper Egyptian Naqada cultures apparently influenced that of Lower Nubia, where Naqada objects have been found in Nubian graves, at sites such as Wadi al-Sebua, Aniba, and Abu Simbel, and the pottery is similar in design.

The A-group (3500–2200 BC)

Between 3500 and 3000 BC, the earliest distinctly Nubian
culture, the A-group, developed in Lower Nubia and the area
immediately north of Aswan. These people were still semi-
nomadic, but toward the end of the fourth millennium they
began to use rock shelters, and permanent settlements became
more common. Agriculture increased, and rearing of livestock
(cattle, sheep, and goats) was practiced to some extent, along
with hunting and fishing. There were close contacts with Egypt
through trade, especially for ebony and ivory. In the First
Cataract region the center for the ivory trade was on the island
of Abu, 'Elephant,' as it was known to the ancient Egyptians,
a name which survives through Greek in the modern name for
the island of Elephantine at Aswan, where this early town was
located. A-group graves contained Egyptian products such as
beer and wine-jars, linen cloth, and Egyptian-style copper
tools. A-group pottery was very attractive, and in general
Nubian ceramics are superior to Egyptian throughout the
pharaonic period. One type of A-group pottery had a polished
red exterior and shiny black interior and rim, while the
'eggshell' pottery, consisting of very thin bowls and cups, was
decorated on the outside with geometric patterns, or basketry
designs, painted in red ocher. Clay figures of humans and
animals were the earliest examples of Nubian sculpture.

After its unification into one kingdom in about 3100 BC,
Egypt developed rapidly under its centralized administration,
with an acceleration in art and architecture, the evolution of a
written language, urbanization, and trade with neighboring
countries. Lower Nubia, however, with its small, scattered
population and largely desert environment, did not develop at
the same pace, and so was an easy target for exploitation by the
Egyptians, who displayed a more aggressive policy toward
Nubia during the Egyptian Old Kingdom (2686–2181 BC). The
diorite quarries west of Toshka were worked more fully, a
fortified town was established at Buhen near the Second
Cataract as a center for the copper industry, canals were cut

through the First Cataract to facilitate passage southward, and Nubians were recruited to fight the Bedouin on the northeast frontier of Egypt. Inscriptions in the tombs of the governors and nobles of Aswan testify to the various trading and mining expeditions into Nubia, one of the most entertaining being that of Harkhuf, who led four trading expeditions to Yam during the reign of Pepi II of the Sixth Dynasty (2278–2184 BC). Yam is presumed to be the area of the Dongola Reach between the Third and Fourth cataracts, which was apparently administered by a ruler with his capital at Kerma. On one of his expeditions Harkhuf acquired a pygmy, which he intended to present to his young sovereign, who was aged about eight years at the time. Having been informed of this gift, the king wrote an excited letter back to Harkhuf with strict instructions to guard the pygmy night and day, so that he should reach Memphis safely. The text of the letter is inscribed beside the entrance of Harkhuf's rock-cut tomb on the west bank of the Nile at Aswan.

The C-group (2200–1570 BC)

Their lives disrupted by the Egyptian policy of exploitation and also by climatic changes, the A-group Nubians retreated to the desert edges and from around 2200 BC a new culture began to establish itself in Lower Nubia, which displayed native elements as well as influences from the southern part of the Western Desert. This C-group culture was able to consolidate its position in Lower Nubia with the breakdown of centralized government in Egypt during the First Intermediate Period (2181–2040 BC), and relations between the two countries appear to have been relatively good. Because of the political disruption in Egypt itself, the Egyptians abandoned the town of Buhen, work ceased at the Toshka quarries, and trade was less aggressive. If trade with areas to the south of the Second Cataract was to continue, it was necessary to maintain good relations with the chiefs of the various districts of Nubia, particularly the up-and-coming kingdom of Kerma south of the Third Cataract. Nubian mercenaries were used by Egyptian governors as security forces during this period of political unrest. Members of a Nubian tribe from the Eastern Desert called the Medjay were particularly favored as soldiers, and later the word 'Medjay' became synonymous with the word for policeman. Nubian bowmen were especially skillful, a reputation which they maintained for many centuries, comparable with the reputation of English archers under Henry V at Agincourt. Mesehti, governor of Asyut around 2000 BC, had a wooden model of a troop of Nubian bowmen buried in his tomb at Asyut, as well as a model of Egyptian infantrymen. These two models are in the Egyptian Museum in Cairo, with a copy of the model of Nubian soldiers in the new Nubia Museum at Aswan.

The C-group people kept large herds of cattle, as well as sheep and goats, and led a more settled way of life. Their pottery was very distinctive and of excellent quality. The black-topped red ware was also associated with Egyptian cultures, but other types showed a strong African influence, such as the bowls decorated with elaborate geometric patterns highlighted with white pigment.

By 2040 BC Egypt was reunited, at the start of the Middle Kingdom. The kings of the Twelfth Dynasty once again looked southward for trade and also to protect their southern frontier against the rising power of the Kerma Culture. Lower Nubia was annexed as a province of Egypt, military campaigns being conducted there by Senusert I and particularly Senusert III, who set up the frontier at Semna, south of the Second Cataract. During the New Kingdom, some five hundred years later, Senusert III was regarded as a patron god of Lower Nubia for his conquest of the region, his name being recorded in several New Kingdom temples, such as Amada. To control Nubia and protect settlements from attacks by desert nomads, the Egyptians built a chain of huge mud-brick fortresses along the Nile at strategic points. These were masterpieces of military architecture, each adapted to suit the terrain of its location, with defensive features such as ramparts, ditches, and drawbridges, which appear many centuries later in medieval castles in Europe, having perhaps been copied by Crusaders from similar fortifications they came across on the northeastern frontier of Egypt. The Nubian fortresses not only guarded important areas of mines and quarries but also served as trading posts, with houses and temples within the walls.

Early in the Twelfth Dynasty the gold mines of Wadi al-Allaqi and Wadi Gabgaba in Lower Nubia were opened up and the nearby fortress of Quban became a center for gold processing and storage; copper ore was also mined in the same area, and the Toshka diorite quarries were reopened. The local C-group people continued to flourish but were suppressed politically by the occupying Egyptians.

The Kerma Culture (1990–1570 BC)

A military buffer zone had thus been created in Lower Nubia between Egypt and the independent Kingdom of Kush, with its capital at Kerma near the Third Cataract. This was one of the earliest urbanized communities in tropical Africa, the first to rival Egypt's position in the area and a power to be reckoned with, as Senusert III tacitly acknowledged on the stela he set up at Semna. The Kerma kingdom, a highly developed society with a king at its head, was located in one of the most fertile stretches of the Nubian Nile Valley, which was clearly an asset. Once again, Lower Nubia became a corridor to Africa, Kerma acting as an entrepot on the great African trade routes that brought ivory, ebony, and various luxury goods to Egypt, and Egyptian products to Kerma in return. Huge brick buildings and skill displayed in jewelry of gold, silver, and faience and in ceramics are all evidence of the prosperity and status of the culture. This is also reflected in the graves, circular tumuli over a burial pit, where the body was surrounded by items for the use of the deceased in the afterlife: leather garments, sandals,

jewelry, food, and weapons. In the exceptionally large royal
tumuli, men, women, and children were sacrificed to
accompany the ruler.

With the Second Intermediate Period in Egypt (1782–1570
BC), when the Delta was taken over by the Asiatic Hyksos, the
Egyptians were forced to withdraw their troops from Lower
Nubia. The Kushites seized the forts at the Second Cataract and
strategic sites as far north as the First Cataract. The Kushites
were allied with the Hyksos in Lower and Middle Egypt, with
only the area around Thebes under Egyptian control. The
Theban princes eventually established themselves as the
Seventeenth Dynasty and succeeded in expelling the Hyksos
from Egypt after a prolonged military campaign.

Nubia during the Egyptian New Kingdom (1570–1070 BC)

Having at last rid themselves of the Hyksos, the Egyptians
were determined to prevent foreign domination occurring
again, and on the pretext of strengthening their borders they
extended Egyptian influence northeastward into Asia and
southward into Nubia, creating an empire that stretched from
the River Euphrates in the north to the Fourth Cataract in the
south. With bitter memories of the alliance between the
Kushites and the Hyksos, the Egyptians were anxious to secure
their back door. Lower Nubia was once more brought under
Egyptian control by the early kings of the Eighteenth
Dynasty, and Tuthmosis I reached and sacked the Kushite
capital at Kerma, advancing as far as the Fourth Cataract. The
Nubians continued to rebel for the next fifty years, but were
finally pacified by Tuthmosis III, who also campaigned in the
region of the Fourth Cataract and founded a new town,
Napata, at Gebel Barkal, to mark Egypt's southern frontier in
Nubia. A temple to Amun, King of the Gods, was built at
Napata, and other temples and shrines were built or renovated
throughout Nubia. Some of the Second Cataract forts, such as
Buhen, were reoccupied as administrative and commercial

centers, new towns were established, and Egyptian culture became widespread.

For the next four hundred years Nubia was a province of Egypt, divided into two parts, Kush in the south and Wawat in the north. The administration was headed by the viceroy, titled the 'King's Son of Kush and Overseer of the Southern Lands,' who was appointed by the pharaoh. He was assisted by two deputies, one for Wawat with his headquarters at Aniba, and one for Kush at Amara. The viceroy was not normally resident in Nubia, his headquarters being at Thebes, but he spent his time traveling through Nubia attending to the various aspects of the administration, the collection of taxes and resources, supervision of building projects, and so on. The deputies resided in their respective centers and were assisted by local Nubian princes, as well as by scribes and overseers. Military affairs also came under the viceroy's jurisdiction, although the armed forces were actually commanded by the 'Troop Commander of Kush.'

During the New Kingdom the gold mines in Lower Nubia were extensively worked, trade goods from central Africa came through Napata, and every year the viceroy presented these to the pharaoh, along with Nubian tribute of local products and resources. This annual presentation is depicted in the tombs of several Theban officials and in Ramesses II's temple of Beit al-Wali. In Lower Nubia, Egyptian customs and dress predominated, to the extent that the culture of the native inhabitants is difficult to identify. Houses, tombs, and manufactured goods were all modeled on Egyptian types. The most important religious site was Napata in the south, with its Holy Mountain and temples to the cult of Amun. Amenophis III built a temple at Soleb in Upper Nubia dedicated to himself as deified king, and a temple to his deified queen, Tiye, at nearby Sedeinga, precedents copied by Ramesses II at Abu Simbel.

Ramesses II was one of the greatest pharaohs of ancient Egypt, who had an exceptionally long reign of sixty-seven years (1279–1212 BC). During this time he conducted several military campaigns in the northeastern part of the Egyptian empire against the Hittites from Anatolia, whose increasing power was threatening the northern limits of Egyptian control. The Battle of Kadesh, fought in the fifth year of Ramesses' reign is probably the most famous battle in Egyptian history. A near disaster for the Egyptian army was averted by the personal courage of the king himself, who subsequently recorded the battle in all his major temples. In Year 21 of his reign he signed a peace treaty with the Hittite king, of which copies have survived from both parties. Ramesses II also left more monuments than any other pharaoh, including the Ramesseum (his mortuary temple in Luxor); the beautiful tomb of his wife, Queen Nefertari, in the Valley of the Queens at Luxor; and the two magnificent temples at Abu Simbel; as well as a new city in the eastern Delta (now reduced to the foundations only). He also built more temples in Nubia than anyone else: at Beit al-Wali, Gerf Hussein, Wadi al-Sebua, Derr, and Abu Simbel, in all of which, apart from Beit al-Wali, he was worshiped as a deified king in his own lifetime, something that usually occurred only after a king's death in his mortuary cult. The raising of the temples at Abu Simbel during the Nubian Rescue Campaign of the 1960s made Ramesses II as well known to the twentieth-century public as Tutankhamun.

Throughout the New Kingdom the population of Lower Nubia was gradually shrinking, whether because of excessive exploitation by the Egyptians or due to a decrease in the agricultural area because of the behavior of the Nile is unknown. As Egypt's grip on its empire in the northeast declined in the eleventh century BC, Nubia suffered the same fate. Gold mining declined, Egyptian settlements were abandoned, and the provincial administration broke down. Events in Nubia are obscure for the following three centuries.

The Napatan Period (760–593 BC)

Nubia came into its own in the eighth century BC, when a new power emerged at Napata and took over Egypt, its kings forming the Egyptian Twenty-fifth Dynasty. The Napatan ruler Kashta gradually extended his control northward as far as the Egyptian border at Aswan. Kashta's successor, Piye (until recently known as Piankhy), seeing Egypt wracked by civil war between rival princes, advanced into Egypt itself, captured Thebes and continued northward, taking cities and the allegiance of their governors. His campaign is recorded on a granite stela that he set up in the Temple of Amun at Gebel Barkal. The text, which names Piye as the King of Egypt and Nubia, chronicles his battles against Tefnakht, the ruler of Sais in the western Delta, who was his main adversary, and is also interesting for his complaints about the mistreatment of horses by the Prince of Khmunu (Ashmunein in Middle Egypt), who left them to starve when his city was besieged. Piye's devotion to the god Amun is stressed, and it is possible that protection of the principal cult center of Amun at Thebes during this period of political upheaval may have been seen by the Nubians as justification for marching on Egypt. Piye's sister, Amenirdis I, was given the title 'God's Wife of Amun' after being adopted in this position by the last Theban holder of the title, Shepenwepet I. The Piye Stela and statues of Amenirdis I are in the newly-opened Nubia Museum in Aswan.

Having taken Memphis, the administrative capital of Egypt, and received the submission of the Delta princes, Piye returned to Nubia, somewhat unwisely leaving the Egyptian authorities to manage their own affairs. Thirteen years later, Piye's successor, Shabako, established firm Kushite control over Egypt based at Thebes and Memphis. The king presided at Memphis, while Upper Egypt was under the authority of the royal princess at Thebes who held the title 'God's Wife of Amun.' The Kushite kings ruled Egypt for about fifty years, political stability promoting a revival in Egyptian art and architecture. The kings styled themselves as pharaohs, adopting Egyptian titles and dress, the Egyptian hieroglyphic script, and burial customs—being interred in pyramids, not in Egypt, but at al-Kurru north of Napata, their Nubian capital. Horse burials were a special feature of these burials, and appear to indicate that there was a particular breed of Nubian horse at this time.

The climax of the Twenty-fifth Dynasty was the reign of the fourth king, Taharka (690–664 BC), who carried out a great deal of building in both Egypt and Nubia. During the second half of his reign his position was repeatedly threatened by Assyrian attempts to invade Egypt. In the first successful invasion, led by Esarhaddon in 671 BC, Memphis was captured and Taharka was forced to flee, while his wife and son were taken prisoner. Taharka regained some hold in Egypt after the Assyrians withdrew, but he was defeated by Ashurbanipal in 667–66 and retreated to Nubia, where he died in 664. The Egyptian princes submitted to the Assyrians, and after the failure of further attempts to reassert control of Egypt by Tantamani, Taharka's successor, the Assyrians sacked Thebes and the Nubian king abandoned Egypt altogether. Egypt came under the rule of the Twenty-sixth Dynasty kings of Sais in the western Delta. In 593 BC Psammetichus II of Egypt made a brief incursion into Nubia, where Greek and Carian mercenaries in his army left graffiti at Abu Simbel. The Nubians moved their capital further south to Meroe, between the Fifth and Sixth cataracts, and Lower Nubia once again became a buffer zone between the two nations.

The Meroitic Period (593 BC – AD 350)

The Meroitic Period of Nubian history was contemporary with the Twenty-seventh to Thirtieth dynasties and the Ptolemaic and Roman periods in Egypt. The kingdom of Meroe flourished from its capital in a fertile strategic location, far removed from the successive invasions taking place in Egypt. In 525 BC the Persians under Cambyses attempted to invade Nubia after their successful takeover of Egypt, but they were defeated and did not have the resources to make a further attempt. The Meroitic sphere of influence gradually expanded, first covering northern Sudan and Upper Nubia, then by the time of King Arkamani (Ergamenes), who was contemporary with Ptolemy IV of Egypt (222–205 BC), as far north as Hierasykaminos (Maharraqa) in Lower Nubia. Under the Ptolemies, the Dodekaschoinos, 'Land of the Twelve Schoinoi' (a schoinos being a Greek distance measurement of approximately eleven kilometers), the part of Lower Nubia between Maharraqa and the First Cataract, which was regarded as the estate of the goddess Isis of Philae, was under Egyptian control. It is possible, however, that Arkamani extended Meroitic rule into this area also, as he and Ptolemy IV collaborated in the building of shrines at Philae and Dakka.

The Meroites controlled several important trade routes from central Africa: northward to Egypt, eastward to the Red Sea, and westward to Kordofan and Darfur. Egyptian influence was strong in Meroitic religion and art, but African and Hellenistic elements were also adopted. Women held an exceptionally high position, especially in the royal family. From 300 BC onward the kings and queens were buried in pyramids at Meroe instead of Napata. A native Meroitic script was developed, Egyptian hieroglyphs being used only for religious purposes. Although the script has been partially deciphered, the Meroitic language is still not completely understood. Excavations of Meroitic sites have produced evidence of their fine work in bronze, textiles, and especially ceramics. As well as coarse utility ware, there are many examples of thin pottery bowls, vases, and cups, decorated with geometric patterns, Egyptian motifs such as the *ankh* and the lotus, vine-leaves (indicating Greco-Roman influence), and animals such as frogs, crocodiles, giraffes, and snakes.

Relations between Nubia and Ptolemaic Egypt were generally good, the expansion of trade in the western Mediterranean by the Macedonian pharaohs creating a demand for exotic goods from the south, such as ivory, spices, animals, and slaves. The Dodekaschoinos was in Egyptian hands because of its strategic importance and access to the Wadi al-Allaqi gold mines, which were reopened during the Ptolemaic Period. Soon after the Romans took over Egypt in 30 BC after the death of

Cleopatra VII, the Meroites came into conflict with the Roman authorities over control of this region. In 23 BC Queen Amanirenas led her army northward and succeeded in occupying Aswan, but she was driven out by the Romans, and eventually the Roman frontier was established at Maharraqa, putting the Dodekaschoinos firmly under Roman control. From then on peace with Rome was maintained, profitable trade resulting. Burials throughout Nubia contained goods imported from Roman Egypt and further afield.

The apex of Meroitic culture was reached by the first century AD, after which there was a long and gradual decline, when the economy became weaker, probably because of competition for Red Sea trade with the Ethiopian kingdom of Axum, a route which was being increasingly used by the Romans in preference to Meroe. Nomadic desert tribes were more mobile after obtaining camels, and increasingly disrupted the lives of Nile Valley communities and trading caravans. In the fourth century AD Meroe was overrun by Noba tribes from the Western Desert. In about 350 Ezana, the first Christian king of Axum, defeated the Noba in battle and gave himself the title 'King of Kasu (Kush),' but in fact the Meroitic kingdom had already disintegrated. The following two centuries are virtually a 'dark age.' The Noba occupied Upper Nubia, while the Nobatae from the Western Desert and the Blemmyes from the Eastern Desert held Lower Nubia.

The Blemmyes, ancestors of the modern Beja, were an aggressive tribe of African origin. From the mid-third century AD they settled in Lower Nubia and even raided north of Aswan into Upper Egypt. The Romans were forced to withdraw their frontier to Aswan at the end of the third century, although the Nobatae formed a buffer between them. Sometimes the Nobatae and Blemmyes opposed each other, at other times they were allies, as, for example, in about 450 when they jointly attacked Philae. In 453 an agreement was made with the Roman authorities allowing the two Nubian tribes to celebrate festivals of Isis in the Temple of Philae, and occasionally to borrow the sacred statue of the goddess, in exchange for keeping the peace. Thus Philae continued in use as a pagan place of worship long after the conversion of the rest of Egypt and the edict of Theodosius I in 394, which made Christianity the official religion of the Byzantine Empire. Philae was finally closed by Justinian in 535, soon after which Silko, the Christian king of the Nobatae, won a victory over the Blemmyes, according to a graffito in the Temple of Kalabsha at Aswan.

The Ballana Culture (fifth and sixth centuries AD)

During the fifth and sixth centuries another new culture developed in Lower Nubia, which is attested over a wide area from Aswan to beyond the Third Cataract. This was originally designated as the 'X-group' but is now called the Ballana Culture, after its most important cemetery. The precise origin of this culture is uncertain: African traditions are traceable, but Meroitic customs were discontinued. The capital may have been at Gebel Adda, a short distance south of Qasr Ibrim. The tombs of kings of this period were discovered at Ballana and Qustul in the 1930s, and contained the richest grave goods ever found in Nubia. Items included jewelry, weapons, furniture, silver crowns inlaid with glass and semiprecious stones, and bronze and silver vessels. Soldiers and servants were buried in the tombs, as well as camels, donkeys, sheep, and horses with saddles and harnesses elaborately decorated with silver.

Christian and Islamic Nubia

By the sixth century Nubia was divided into three kingdoms: the kingdom of Nobatia from the First to the Third Cataract, the kingdom of Makuria to the south as far as the Fifth Cataract, and the kingdom of Alwa further south in the region of the earlier Meroitic kingdom. Christianity gradually began to spread through Nubia from the fifth century onward, brought by merchants, monks, and other travelers. In 543 Nobatia was officially converted to Christianity, and by 569 the kingdoms of Makuria and Alwa had also been converted.

In 640 Egypt became a part of the expanding Arab empire and in 652 a treaty was made between the Muslims and Christian Nubia, which established trading relations and kept the peace for the next five hundred years. In about 700 the kingdoms of Nobatia and Makuria united, increasing prestige and trade in the region. The twelfth and thirteenth centuries saw a decline in the fortunes of Christian Nubia, accelerated by the attack on Nubia, in 1173, by Turan Shah, the brother of Saladin, in retaliation for the Nubians' support of his brother's Fatimid opponents. The fortress town of Qasr Ibrim was raided and parts of it destroyed. Peace was reestablished soon afterward between Nubia and Egypt, but Nubia was increasingly being threatened by Western Desert tribes who were Muslims. Internal unrest and conflict with the Mamluks, who had risen to power in Egypt, caused a total breakdown in administration. In 1315, Kerenbes, the last Christian king of Nubia, was replaced by the Arabs with a Muslim ruler, and the majority of the population converted to Islam. Nubia no longer had political power and reverted to its role as a transit route to the southern Nile Valley and central Africa.

Early in the sixteenth century the mysterious Fung dynasty from the southeast, whose origins are still obscure, conquered Alwa and made their capital at Sennar on the Blue Nile. They advanced northward into Lower Nubia, which was occupied by the Ottoman Turks, who had taken over Egypt in 1517 and installed a garrison of Bosnian mercenaries at Qasr Ibrim. The Turks recognized Fung authority as far north as the Third Cataract. Apart from Ibrim and a few other strongholds occupied by the Turks, archaeological finds from Nubia over the next three hundred years are scarce. In 1805 Muhammad Ali came to power in Egypt and between 1820 and 1825 sent armies to annex Nubia and Sudan, including the now much weakened Fung kingdom of Sennar, eventually making them provinces of the Ottoman Empire. This opened the way for traders and adventurers of all kinds to travel to Nubia, and a brisk trade in elephant tusks and slaves ensued. By 1881 support for the religious leader, the Mahdi, was gaining support in Sudan, culminating in the massacre of the British general Gordon and his troops in Khartoum in 1885, Egypt having become a British Protectorate in 1882. In 1889 the Mahdi and his forces invaded Nubia but were defeated at Toshka, and in 1898 Sudan was retaken by Egyptian forces with British officers, led by Kitchener. The following year the joint Anglo-Egyptian government of Sudan was established, and the border between Egypt and Sudan was set at Adindan, about forty kilometers north of Wadi Halfa. Sudan became independent in 1956, and the ancient land of Nubia was irrevocably split.

Egyptian Nubia in Modern Times

Napoleon's expedition to Egypt in 1798, although a military disaster from his point of view, opened up Egypt and Nubia to the attention of Europeans. Napoleon brought with him to Egypt a group of historians, artists, and other specialists, who traveled in the wake of his army to investigate and record the fabled monuments of the land of the pharaohs. A thorough survey was made of the ancient monuments and all aspects of contemporary life: the flora and fauna, geography, traditions of the inhabitants, racial types, and so on. Nubia was included, and the differences between the Nubians and the Egyptians in language, customs, appearance, and many other details were noted. The results of the scholars' prodigious work were published in 1809 in the *Description de l'Egypte*. After the assumption of power in Egypt in 1805 by Muhammad Ali, who welcomed European scholars and entrepreneurs, several came to Nubia, including in 1813 the Swiss explorer Johann Ludwig Burckhardt, who studied the local people and their society, as well as the ancient monuments, and was the first to discover the Great Temple at Abu Simbel. In 1817, the Italian engineer Giovanni Belzoni, employed by Henry Salt, the

British consul general in Cairo, to collect antiquities, also sailed south of Aswan into Nubia, keeping a record of his journey. Knowing of the temple of Ramesses II at Abu Simbel from Burckhardt, he managed to clear enough sand from the entrance to explore the interior.

Egypt was now included in the Grand Tour and became a favorite venue for the more adventurous traveler, as well as artists and antiquaries, such as the Scottish painter David Roberts, Florence Nightingale, the French draftsman Prisse d'Avennes, the writer Flaubert with his photographer companion Maxime du Camp, and Amelia Edwards, who founded the Egypt Exploration Fund (now the Egypt Exploration Society) in London. These, and many others who traveled through Egypt to Nubia and the Sudanese border, wrote lively accounts of their adventures and the places they visited.

The observation made by the Greek historian Herodotus, when he visited Egypt in the fifth century BC, that Egypt is 'the gift of the river,' is just as true today as it was 2,500 years ago. The only change since then is that nature has been restrained, and the rise and fall of the Nile in Egypt and Sudan are now under human control. However, in Egypt, where 96 percent of the country is desert and the Nile is the only major water source, the river is still the lifeblood of the land and its people.

The volume of water in the Nile increases during the summer months, as a result of rainfall in the Ethiopian highlands. Before the building of the dams at Aswan, the river flooded the agricultural areas of Egypt from June to October, and using a basin system of irrigation by digging dikes and ditches at the start of the inundation season the Egyptians were able to irrigate land, such as the desert edges, which was a long way from the river, and to grow at least two crops as the river level dropped again. Another benefit was the rich alluvial silt, which was brought down by the flood and deposited on the land as the water receded, so the fertility of the soil was replenished each year. The inundation was such an important event in the lives of the ancient Egyptians that its rise marked the start of a new year.

As the flood was a natural phenomenon, however, it did not always reach the ideal level. Both a low flood and a high flood could cause poor harvests and possible starvation. With a low flood, there was insufficient water and silt; with a high flood, the water ran away too quickly so very little silt was deposited, houses could be washed away, and livestock and sometimes people drowned. The ideal rise was about 7 to 8 meters. Very early in their history the Egyptians learned to observe the gradual rise of the flood and to make provision for its consequences, and in years of plenty, grain was stored up against years of want.

Toward the end of the nineteenth century, the Egyptian government was faced with a marked increase in the population, as well as the problems resulting from the annual Nile flood, which not only rendered the agricultural areas unusable for three to four months every summer but was also unpredictable. The decision was taken, therefore, to build a dam across the First Cataract at Aswan to harness the waters of the Nile and regulate irrigation, which was particularly important for the cotton growing industry. However, technological expertise at that time could not provide a dam that would retain the extra volume of water remaining from successive floods, so although the first Aswan Dam saw the end of the basin irrigation system in Egypt, it could not store the flood water from one year to the next. Consequently, more water was released in the early summer to make way for the flood, and over 30 billion cubic meters of water was lost into the Mediterranean each year.

The Aswan Dam was designed by the British engineer Sir William Willcocks and built between 1898 and 1902. It was constructed of Aswan granite, with 180 sluice gates for the release of water, a hydroelectric power station to produce power for industry, and a navigational canal with four locks at the western end to allow for the passage of boats. At 30 meters high and almost two kilometers long, it was the largest dam in the world at that time, and the longest until the building of the High Dam at Aswan.

On completion of the dam, the Nile Valley south of Aswan was flooded as far as Wadi al-Sebua, a distance of about 160 kilometers. As the capacity of the dam proved inadequate, it was heightened twice, in 1912 and 1934, resulting in a final length of 2.14 kilometers, a height of 42 meters, and a width of 30 meters at the base, 7 meters at the top.

With the building of the Aswan Dam, and particularly after its subsequent heightening, when the reservoir extended as far as Wadi Halfa and the water level rose from 87 to 121 meters, many of the ancient monuments in Lower Nubia were partially under water for the greater part of the year, except for a few months during the summer. Archaeological surveys of Nubia were conducted before the two heightenings of the dam, and consolidation work was carried out on several ancient temples to strengthen them, when it was realized that they would be submerged over a prolonged period each year from then on.

In the 1930s a large proportion of the Nubian villages along the Nile were totally submerged. Some Nubians decided to move north into Egypt, where the government allowed them to purchase land, and they built new villages modeled on the domestic architecture of their homeland. The majority, however, chose to stay in their doomed country, and rebuilt their houses on higher ground above the new shoreline. Unfortunately, extensive date palm orchards, which were a mainstay of the Nubian economy, and vanished agricultural land could not be replaced quickly, which resulted in social changes, as many Nubian men left home to seek work, especially in Egypt, where they have always enjoyed a reputation of being particularly reliable and honest. The women were left behind with the children and the elderly to run their communities, where they played a very important role in managing their domestic economy and family life, as their menfolk came home only for brief visits at long intervals.

By the 1950s it had become obvious that a new dam was needed at Aswan. Egypt's population had more than doubled since the building of the first dam, rising from nine million in 1897 to twenty million in 1947, and it was realized that agricultural production would no longer be able to keep pace with this rate of increase, which was set to continue because of improved health care, lower infant mortality, and longer life expectancy.

After the revolution in 1952 it also became imperative for the new regime under Gamal Abd al-Nasser to provide for the population by improving their living conditions and preventing problems caused by the Nile flood. The decision to build the High Dam was taken in 1954, and a German plan was adopted. Substantial financial assistance was to be provided by various Western powers, but when this offer was withdrawn in 1956 because of Nasser's refusal to stop buying arms from the Eastern bloc, Nasser nationalized the Suez Canal, and the Soviet Union provided assistance with a credit system and two thousand engineers and technicians, the thirty-thousand-strong labor force consisting of Egyptians.

The foundation stone for the new dam was laid in January 1960 by President Nasser, and it was officially inaugurated by President Sadat in January 1971.

The High Dam, situated seven kilometers above the old Aswan Dam, consists of a clay core with rock and sand fill and concrete facing, containing seventeen times the volume of material of the Great Pyramid at Giza. The dam is 3.6 kilometers long, 111 meters high, 980 meters wide at its base, and 40 meters wide at the top. There is a hydroelectric power station at the eastern end of the dam with twelve turbines producing 2.1 million kilowatts per hour. The dam is impassable to shipping, as it has no navigational canal or locks.

When the High Dam was completed, the reservoir, now known as Lake Nasser, stretched southward to an overall length of 510 kilometers, one-third of which is in Sudan. The width of the lake varies between five and 35 kilometers, with an average width of ten kilometers; it has a surface area of 5,250 square kilometers, and a maximum capacity of 157 billion cubic meters, with allowance for an exceptionally high flood through the provision of a spillway at Toshka. The average level of the lake surface is approximately 182 meters above sea-level.

Much debate has been entered into since the completion of the High Dam as to the adverse consequences of its construction. These include the increased salinity of the land, due to the higher water table, which is not only detrimental to agriculture but is also affecting the ancient monuments, which suck up the ground water by capillary action, resulting in the crumbling away of relief carvings and painted wall surfaces. The sardine industry on the Mediterranean coast has declined dramatically, because the alluvial silt off which the fish used to feed is no longer carried down by the annual flood. The northern coastline of Egypt is also suffering serious erosion for the same reason. The bilharzia parasite has increased in the now perennially full irrigation canals, and the effects of prolonged use of chemical fertilizers in the absence of the fertile silt have still to be fully analyzed.

However, taken overall, the advantages do seem to outweigh the disadvantages: irrigation can now be satisfactorily regulated, hydroelectric power for much of Egypt's industry is produced relatively cheaply, and in the 1980s, when southern Sudan suffered almost a decade of the most terrible drought, the High Dam reservoir saved Egypt from suffering similar consequences.

With the decision to build the High Dam, it was realized by Egypt and Sudan, and the archaeological world as a whole, that much of the world's cultural heritage from Nubia would be lost for ever unless action was taken. After urgent appeals by both countries, UNESCO sponsored the Nubian Rescue Campaign from 1960 to 1980, in which fifty countries took part, providing financial contributions as well as archaeologists, engineers, and expertise of every kind. Wherever feasible, monuments were dismantled or cut from the rock and reassembled at new sites in Egypt and Sudan. Cemeteries and structures that could not be moved, such as the great mud-brick fortresses, were excavated and recorded in as much detail as possible. Egypt gave five ancient monuments to five countries in recognition of their contributions to the rescue efforts.

Other inevitable victims of the submersion of Nubia were the Nubians themselves, who not only lost their homes and the land of their forebears but were also in danger of losing their unique Nubian identity. The Nubians were of different ethnic groups in Lower, Middle, and Upper Nubia, each with their own language, although the inhabitants of Middle Nubia near the Sudanese border spoke Arabic. The Nubian languages are still something of a mystery, as they seem to be unrelated to other linguistic groups in the area. They are still only spoken languages, with no script of their own. Nubian houses were made of adobe and stone with vaulted and domed roofs in Lower Nubia near Aswan, and flat roofs of split palm trunks and branches further south. The houses, which were whitewashed or covered with mud-plaster, were decorated inside and out by the women and children with colorful pictures of birds, animals, flowers, and flags, often with ceramic plates set into the wall, the entrances displaying elaborate lattice-work in mud-brick. A typical Nubian house has been built in the garden of the Nubia Museum at Aswan. In the 1960s fifty thousand Egyptian Nubians were rehoused in the Kom Ombo area north of Aswan in villages built by the government. Fifty-three thousand Sudanese Nubians were moved even further away from their original homeland, to Khasm al-Girba on the Atbara River, over 1000 kilometers south of Wadi Halfa.

It is a surprise to many people who make the cruise on Lake Nasser that so little appears to have been done over the past twenty-five to thirty years to develop the shores of the lake with new villages, agricultural areas, or even tourist centers. Several factors have to be taken into consideration in this regard, including the lack of any infrastructure to support such communities, the provision of which would be a very costly undertaking, and the fluctuating level of the lake, dependent on rainfall in the uplands of Ethiopia, which can vary considerably.

New villages have been developed near the site of old Kalabsha, at Abu Simbel, and near the Sudanese border. Small fishing communities have also sprung up along the lake and more are planned. It was originally calculated that the alluvial silt would take about five hundred years to build up before the amount became a problem, and it was believed that it would settle near to the dam, but it is actually accumulating 95 to 130 kilometers further south. Future technology will no doubt eventually find a cost-effective way to extract this valuable agricultural material, thus facilitating land reclamation in the region.

When the High Dam was under construction, a spillway was made at Toshka about thirty kilometers north of Abu Simbel, which could be opened up if the water level in the lake became dangerously high. This spillway was opened for the first time in 1996 by President Mubarak, in a ceremony reminiscent of the ancient pharaonic ceremony to celebrate the beginning of the annual Nile flood. An ambitious scheme is now underway to water the Nubian desert between Toshka and the New Valley, irrigating thousands of acres of land by means of a new canal, to build several new cities, and to provide homes and livelihood for millions of people—in other words, the rebirth of Lower Nubia.

New Kalabsha

The site of New Kalabsha on the western side of Lake Nasser, one kilometer south of the Aswan High Dam, contains the temples of Kalabsha and Beit al-Wali, the Kiosk of Qertassi, and the Chapel of Dedwen, all of which were moved here from their original locations further south during the UNESCO campaign. The area is reached nowadays by motor launch from the western end of the High Dam beside the fish-canning factory. New Kalabsha is included in the sightseeing program of the Lake Nasser cruise ships, which moor in the harbor at the eastern end of the High Dam and use their own launches to transport visitors to the site.

The Temple of Kalabsha (plan 1, page 90)

The Temple of Kalabsha, the largest Nubian temple after the rock-cut Great Temple of Abu Simbel and the largest free-standing one, stood fifty kilometers south at ancient Talmis, which is now submerged. The city of Talmis was situated on both sides of the Nile at a point where the river narrowed, giving the area its name Bab al-Kalabsha, the Gate of Kalabsha. The temple was built in the time of the Roman emperor Augustus, in the last century BC, presumably on the site of an earlier temple of the Eighteenth Dynasty, as Amenophis II (1453–1419 BC) is depicted in the pillared hall, and a black granite statue of Tuthmosis III (1504–1450 BC) was observed near the river bank in the last century, although its

whereabouts is now unknown. An unspecified Ptolemaic
pharaoh is also depicted on the same wall as Amenophis III,
which indicates that the temple was rebuilt sometime in the
Ptolemaic Period, although the decoration all appears to date
from the Roman era.

The temple was dismantled by a West German team and the
13,000 blocks of sandstone were reerected at the present site
between 1961 and 1963. In front of the building to the east is
an extensive causeway (A) over thirty meters in length leading
to a quayside that provided the approach from the river. At the
western end of the causeway are steps rising up to the terrace
on which the temple stands.

The temple was dedicated to Mandulis (Egyptian, Merwel),
a Lower Nubian sun god, who is here equated with Horus and
so is associated with Osiris and Isis. He is usually shown in
human form wearing an elaborate crown of ram's horns,
cobras, and plumes topped with sun disks, but he is also
occasionally depicted with a man's head on a falcon's body.
Throughout the temple (especially in the two vestibules and
the sanctuary), Mandulis appears with Wadjet, the patron
goddess of Lower Egypt, whose cult center was at Buto in the
western Delta. In several examples they are joined by a young
form of Mandulis, making a triad, or holy family, virtually
equated with the triad of Osiris, Isis, and Horus, frequently
depicted on the same wall, or in the parallel position on the
opposite wall.

The carved relief decoration of the various parts of the
temple was not completed, except in the innermost chambers,
and in several places there are roughly carved graffiti of
different figures, especially falcons. On the reliefs in general, the
comment has been made that the figures seem to have a Nubian
look about them, inconsistent with representations in other
Greco-Roman temples. Before the raising of the old Aswan
Dam and the temple's partial submersion for several months of
the year, there was apparently a considerable amount of color
preserved in the rear portion. The application of the color,
however, evidently left something to be desired, and Amelia

Edwards, an artist herself, visiting in 1873, was especially critical: "Such a masquerade of deities; such striped and spotted and cross-barred robes; such outrageous head-dresses; such crude and violent coloring, we have never seen the like of." Perhaps we are lucky that the colors have now disappeared!

The impressive pylon (B) is set slightly askew to the east–west axis of the temple and the causeway. It is well preserved except for the cornice, but is undecorated apart from the doorway and the winged sun-disk above it. On the right-hand side of the entrance passage (1) the emperor Augustus is shown before Horus. Coptic graffiti and crosses can be seen by the doorway, indicating the temple's later reuse as a Christian church.

This temple follows the standard plan, also to be seen at Edfu, with a monumental pylon followed by an open court, hypostyle (pillared) hall, and vestibules preceding the sanctuary. The open court at Kalabsha (C) had a colonnade with fourteen columns on the north, east, and south sides, but only the columns on the north and south sides still stand up to their original height and display the complex floral designs that are characteristic of temples of the Greco-Roman Period. The designs of the capitals are arranged in pairs facing each across the court. The two at the far end on the left and right represent palm branches with bunches of dates hanging underneath. There is no decoration on the walls of the open court. Doorways in the pylon towers give access to staircases to the roof and two small chambers on each side, and there are also four small chambers cut in the thickness of the north and south walls, which were probably used as storerooms.

On the far side of the open court is the pronaos (D), the forepart of the temple proper, the façade of which consists of four columns joined by screen-walls. The decoration of the façade was incomplete, only the two screen-walls on the south side having carved scenes. The one immediately to the left of the door (3) shows the king being purified by Horus and Thoth, who are pouring over the king sacred water that is represented by streams of the hieroglyphic signs for 'life' and 'dominion.' On the opposite side of the façade are some interesting graffiti, as well as some roughly carved figures. On the first screen-wall to the right of the doorway (4), above a damaged scene of the king before Mandulis and Isis, is an inscription in Greek by the Roman governor of Ombos and Elephantine, Aurelius Besarion (c. 248 AD), ordering the temple to be cleared of pigs. On the second column on the right (5), between two Greek votive texts, is a long inscription in Meroitic cursive script of the Blemmye king Kharamadeye (fourth century AD). The most interesting graffito is on the right-hand end of the façade (7), an inscription in bad Greek by Silko, the Christian king of the Nubian kingdom of Nobatia (fifth or sixth century AD), commemorating his victory over the Blemmyes. Near this inscription is a rough carving of a man in Roman dress on horseback spearing a prostrate enemy and being crowned by a winged Victory. This is reminiscent of Coptic representations of warrior saints on horseback, such as can be seen painted in some of the older Coptic churches in Egypt.

The doorway to the hypostyle hall beyond has scenes of Isis with Mandulis and other gods. The hypostyle hall (D) has eight columns, their floral capitals now in a damaged condition. Most of this part of the temple was left undecorated, but there are signs of its later use as a Christian church, where crosses have been carved on the walls, especially to the left of the doorway (9). On the west side is the entrance to the inner section of the building, the façade of which has four registers of scenes carved in raised relief on each side with a procession of the king followed by Nile gods before Mandulis at the bottom of each wall. Scenes in the second register from the top on the south side (10) are noteworthy, as they indicate the earlier history of the temple. The scene on the left shows an unspecified Ptolemy offering a field to Isis, Mandulis, and Horus, while the scene on the right depicts Amenophis II offering wine to Min-Re and Mandulis. On the north wall (11) in the fourth register, Mandulis, recognizable by his crown, is depicted in the form of a falcon with a human head, in a clump of lotuses in a scene with an unnamed king offering to him and Isis. This recalls the legend of Isis, who hid her infant son, Horus, in the Delta marshes to protect him from Seth, his father's murderer and rival for the throne of Egypt. The inscriptions on this wall were not completed. On the lintel of the doorway the Roman emperor Trajan appears in a double scene offering to Mandulis, Osiris, and Isis.

The two vestibules and the sanctuary each originally had two columns supporting the roof, but these are no longer in place. The roof has been reconstructed to preserve the reliefs, but unfortunately this part of the temple is not illuminated, so each room is darker than the last, as the limited amount of daylight that filters in through the doorways and the narrow skylights is insufficient to light all the walls, even on a sunny day. This is especially the case in the sanctuary. However, as you approach the sanctuary, where the divine image was kept, the increasing darkness does give an impression of mystery, which was a deliberate architectural device of the ancient builders, to emphasize the god's mystical presence.

The decoration of the outer vestibule (E) is incomplete, especially on the south wall, which is of interest in demonstrating how the ancient artists carried out their work. The unfinished state of the scenes also produces some amusing incidents, which provide some much-needed light relief among the tedious offering scenes. One such occurs in the third register at the west end of the south wall (14), where Thoth and Horus are purifying a headless king!

At the bottom of the walls is a procession of nome-gods headed by the emperor, before Osiris, Isis, and Horus on the south side of the room (13, 14, 15), and before Mandulis, young Mandulis, and Wadjet on the north side (16, 17, 18). The frieze at the top of the walls includes the cartouches of Augustus. On the left side of the room is a staircase leading to the roof, where another staircase descends to two small chambers and a crypt in the thickness of the south wall of the inner vestibule. These may have been connected with the cult of Osiris, but are undecorated and are not accessible to visitors.

Further steps go up to the roof of the hypostyle hall, from which there is a good view of the nearby Kiosk of Qertassi, and the lake.

The inner vestibule (F) is similar to the outer one in size, style, and decoration, although the scenes here are complete. Among the gods depicted are some of interest, such as the lion-headed Tutu, a god of the Late Period also worshiped in Dakhla Oasis in the Western Desert, and Imhotep, the chief minister and architect of King Djoser of the Third Dynasty, who was deified in the Greco-Roman Period as a god of wisdom and medicine (both on the south wall, 21). On the east wall, north side (23), can be seen Arsenuphis and Tefnut, principal deities in the Greco-Roman temple of Dakka, while on the north wall (24, upper register), the emperor offers a Maat figure to two Nubian forms of Amun, of Napata, the first capital of the Kingdom of Meroe, and of Primis, the Roman name for Qasr Ibrim. The procession at the bottom of the walls is the same as in the outer vestibule. On the left is a small, undecorated chamber and a passage giving access to the sanctuary (G).

Above the doorway to the sanctuary is the winged sun-disk, with inscriptions on the jambs. The scenes in the sanctuary run in opposite directions on each side of the chamber, those on the north side anti-clockwise, on the south clockwise, meeting in the center of the back wall. Two columns also originally supported the roof. The emperor is again depicted with various gods, Mandulis, Wadjet, Osiris, Isis, and Horus occurring most frequently. The procession at the base of the walls is similar to that in the two vestibules, showing the emperor with Nile gods offering to Osiris and Mandulis on the south side (27, 28, 29), and to Isis and Mandulis on the north (30, 31, 32).

An outer corridor, or ambulatory, runs around the main part of the temple, access to which is either from the north and south ends of the colonnade in the open court or from doorways on the north and south sides of the hypostyle hall. On the back wall of the temple itself, the exterior wall of the sanctuary (33), is a large, double scene of the king with deities, with some roughly carved figures underneath. On the outer wall of the corridor opposite (34), is a relief of the king before Mandulis with an offering-stand between them. The crown on the king's head is an unusual depiction of the double crown shown face on, although the figure is in profile. It is interesting to see that the eyes of the two figures on this wall, and that of Mandulis on the wall opposite, have been deeply cut to take inlay and so make the eyes look more lifelike. It was common practice in ancient Egypt for artists to inlay the eyes of statues with a copper frame and ivory and polished stone, but this technique is seen only rarely in temple reliefs. Grooves and holes above and on each side of this scene (34) suggest that a wooden canopy fitted into the wall around the scene to give the appearance of a shrine, where perhaps common people could make their private prayers. Kalabsha was apparently a healing temple like Kom Ombo and Edfu, where those suffering from various serious ailments would come to spend the night in the outer corridor of the temple, presumably in the hope of being miraculously cured. On the south side of the corridor is a circular Nilometer (H), now well above the water level, with a staircase going down beside it. Nilometers were used by the ancient Egyptians to measure the gradual rise of the annual Nile flood in the summertime, first of all so that word could be sent northward regarding the possible limit of the flood, which would indicate the amount of work needed making channels and dikes to control the extra water. Secondly, tax assessors were able to make a preliminary estimate of the revenue to be gained from the harvest the following spring, based on the eventual predicted height of the inundation. Evidently tax-men have always worked in mysterious ways!

Behind the temple to the southwest is a chapel (I) consisting of a small rock-cut chamber enclosed by a forecourt of granite pillars with screen-walls. Only the doorway of the chamber is decorated and has reliefs of an unnamed pharaoh offering to the Nubian god Dedwen. As this chapel was originally inside the mud-brick enclosure wall of the temple

precincts, it may have served as a birth-house. To the northeast
of the temple pylon is a small, unfinished chapel of the
Ptolemaic Period from the reign of Ptolemy IX (K), which
therefore predates the larger temple. The exterior of the chapel
is undecorated, but reliefs inside show the king offering to the
Triad of Elephantine, Khnum, Satis, and Anukis, as well as to
Mandulis, Wadjet, Osiris, Isis, and Horus. On the north side
of the temple is a granite stela of Psammetichus II of the
Twenty-sixth Dynasty (J), recording his successful Nubian
campaign in 593 BC. On the south side (L) are several
prehistoric petroglyphs dating from 5000 to 3000 BC, which
were also brought from further south and show various
animals, such as elephants and gazelle. Nearby, in four pieces, is
a rock-cut stela of Seti I from Qasr Ibrim, and a few blocks
with carved reliefs from the temple of Ramesses II at Gerf
Hussein, which could not be saved *in toto*. A pillar from the
same temple, fronted by a colossal statue of the king, with two
architrave blocks bearing the titles of Ramesses II, forms the
impressive centerpiece in the main hall of the new Nubia
Museum at Aswan.

When the Temple of Kalabsha was dismantled, blocks from
a small Ptolemaic shrine and a gateway were discovered in the
foundations. The former, which has reliefs of Ptolemy IX and
Augustus Caesar, has been reconstructed on the southern end
of Elephantine Island in Aswan, while the latter is now in the
Ägyptische Museum in Berlin, having been given to Germany
by the Egyptian government in gratitude for the moving and
rebuilding of the temple.

The Kiosk of Qertassi

A short distance to the south of the Temple of Kalabsha is the
charming kiosk of Qertassi, brought here by the Egyptian
Antiquities Organization from forty kilometers further south,
where it stood at the entrance to ancient sandstone quarries.
This Nubian gem was situated on high ground overlooking the

Nile and was a landmark for miles around. It was described poetically by Weigall in 1910: "The ruin, outlined against the rocks, forms a picture of the greatest charm." Something of that old charm has been recaptured in its present location.

Hathor was the patron goddess of miners and quarrymen, and two Hathor-headed columns flank the entrance. Near the kiosk at its original site was a rock-cut shrine to Isis and a local form of Osiris. The kiosk consists of a single chamber, formed by four columns with exceptionally fine floral capitals, with screen-walls between them (that on the south side is destroyed). The main entrance is on the north side, and there is another doorway on the west side. The kiosk was originally roofed with sandstone blocks, but these are no longer in place. The concept is similar in design, though on a smaller scale, to Trajan's Kiosk at Philae. No dates were found at the quarries earlier than the Ptolemaic Period, to which the Kiosk of Qertassi can therefore almost certainly be assigned. This supposition is reinforced by the composite nature of the capitals and the style of the only piece of relief in the kiosk, which is on the upper part of the northwest column and shows the king before Isis and Horus the Child (Greek, Harpocrates). It has been suggested that the Kiosk of Qertassi, along with the small Greco-Roman temples of Dabod and Dendur, was a processional way-station on the route taken by the image of the goddess Isis of Philae through northern Lower Nubia (the Dodekaschoinos), which formed her estate.

The Temple of Beit al-Wali *(plan 2, page 94)*

Before the Nubian Rescue Campaign, the small rock-cut temple of Beit al-Wali was located in a side valley a short distance to the northwest of the Temple of Kalabsha. It is now at New Kalabsha, where it was reconstructed in a rocky hillside in the same position relative to Kalabsha Temple as it was previously. In spite of its size and reasonably good state of preservation, the decoration in the Temple of Kalabsha is hardly a feast for

the eyes. However, in the Beit al-Wali temple of Ramesses II
(1279–1212 BC), the historical scenes in the forecourt and the
good quality relief with much color preserved in the inner part
of the temple make it a joy to visit. The more selective
representations of gods and goddesses and the relative
simplicity of its decoration scheme also add to its appeal, after
an overdose of deities in the Roman temple.

It is not immediately clear to whom the temple was
dedicated, but Amun-Re is depicted most frequently and so
seems the most likely candidate. Other gods represented include
Khnum, the god of Elephantine, and his two consorts, Satis
and Anukis; the goddess Mut, consort of Amun-Re; and
Nubian forms of the god Horus. Like most of the Nubian
temples, Beit al-Wali also ended its days as a Christian church,
where the forecourt comprised the nave of the church, which
was covered with brick-built domes. The Arabic name for the
temple, Beit al-Wali, by which it is now normally known,
means 'the house of the holy man,' so it is possible that this
small shrine was in fact a Christian hermit's dwelling at some
stage.

The temple consists of a stone gateway set in a brick wall, a
forecourt, a vestibule with two columns and a sanctuary.
Ramesses II is carved in sunk relief on either side of the
gateway (A) as if to welcome visitors. In the forecourt (B) the
lower part of the walls was cut out of the rock and the court
was roofed with a brick barrel-vault over a wooden frame.
Today the lower rock-cut section of the walls is the only part
that survives, but a few courses of the upper brick part have
been reconstructed in new bricks to give an idea of how the
upper part of the side-walls looked. The brick vault must have
been similar to those that roof the magazines behind the
Ramesseum, the mortuary temple of Ramesses II on the West
Bank in Luxor.

The most interesting scenes in the temple are those on the
north and south walls of the forecourt, which depict Ramesses
II's campaigns against the Nubians, the Syrians, and the
Libyans in the early years of his reign, when he was co-regent

with his father, Seti I. Early last century, J. Bonomi took plaster casts of the reliefs, unfortunately removing some of the original color by doing so. However, he had made detailed notes of the colors so that the casts could be painted, and these are on display in the British Museum.

Following the usual practice in Egyptian temples of positioning historical scenes according to their geographical orientation, the scenes dealing with the Nubians are on the south wall, and those concerning the Asiatics and Libyans on the north. The scenes at the east end on each wall are more damaged than those at the west end, but overall they give a lively account of the young king's activities. The carving on the south wall of the forecourt and the eastern half of the north wall is in sunk relief, and at the western end of the north wall and in the inner part of the temple it is in raised relief. It is strange that the type of relief changes part way along the north wall; it is assumed that the original intention was that all the carving should be in raised relief, and then before the forecourt was completed, the order was changed, possibly so that the decoration could be finished more quickly, as sunk relief, where the figures are cut into the surface, is probably less time-consuming than raised relief, where the surface is cut away so that the figures stand out. Near the middle of the south wall (3) Ramesses II in his chariot charges vigorously against a band of Nubians, while shooting with his bow, the horses' reins tied around his waist. Behind him, his eldest son, Prince Amenhirwenemef, and his fourth son, Khaemwaset, are following in their own chariots, each with a driver. The boys were being introduced to the arts of warfare at an early age, as they were only about six and four years old at the time! Prince Amenhirwenemef, who later had his name changed to Amenhirkhopshef, the form in which it appears at Abu Simbel from the twenty-fourth year of his father's reign, eventually predeceased his father. He was the son of Queen Nefertari, Ramesses' first Chief Wife and perhaps his favorite, for whom the king built the smaller temple at Abu Simbel and a magnificent tomb in the Valley of the Queens in Thebes.

Khaemwaset was the son of Ramesses' second Chief Wife, Isetnofret, and in adulthood became famous as a sage and a magician, especially at Memphis, where he was High Priest of the Temple of Ptah. It was another son of Queen Isetnofret, Merenptah, the thirteenth son of Ramesses II, who eventually succeeded his father as pharaoh, his twelve older brothers having predeceased their father.

The Nubians, armed with bows and arrows, are fleeing in panic, back to their camp among the doum-palms. Two men half-carry a wounded comrade, women and children are running about in confusion, and one woman is cooking over a fire (top left). The scenes of the Nubian camp are now difficult to identify without a certain amount of concentration, but the doum-palm with its divided trunk, large round 'leaves' and bunches of doum nuts is easy to recognize, as well as a few of the Nubians. At the west end of the same wall, the king is seated in a pavilion to receive the tribute of the Nubians, which is being presented to him in two registers by Prince Amenhirwenemef and the viceroy of Kush, Amenemope son of Paser. In the upper register the viceroy is being rewarded with collars of gold disks, as he was responsible for the collection of the tribute. The gifts include leopard skins, gold rings and bags of gold dust, bows, shields, chairs, ebony and elephants' tusks, as well as ostrich eggs, feathers, and fans. Animals are also being brought, including cattle, gazelle, a lion (upper register), two leopards, a giraffe, monkeys, and an ostrich (all in the lower register). Interesting details can be observed; for example, at the left of the lower register a woman is carrying her two children in a basket on her back with the strap of the basket around her forehead. One of the bulls in the same register has horns in the shape of two arms with a Nubian head between them. Cattle are occasionally shown with oddly-shaped horns, especially those being presented as tribute, or as sacrificial beasts for a temple. In Luxor Temple, for example, there is a scene in the open court showing cattle being presented to the temple, where one has horns just like these with the Nubian head. The horns were artificially distorted, and cattle with such horns were pparently considered to be particularly valuable. It is still not lear whether this was originally an Egyptian or a Nubian ustom, although the latter seems more likely.

There are five scenes on the north wall (4). Taking the scenes rom right to left, The first scene at the east end of the wall, vhich is partly damaged, shows the king trampling on two Asiatic enemies, while holding three more by the hair in his left and and brandishing an ax with his right. On the right of the cene Prince Amenhirwenemef leads in one Libyan and three yrian captives. In the second scene the king and the prince ttack a Syrian fortress; some of the defenders are falling from he battlements, while others are appealing to the king. The hird scene has an animated picture of Ramesses, wearing the ed crown of Lower Egypt, charging Bedouin in his chariot. As e leans down from his chariot, he has his left leg over the ront of it, with his foot on the shaft, the horses' reins around is waist, and still manages to hold some captives in his left and, while wielding his scimitar in his right! Continuing to he left, the next scene depicts the king smiting a Libyan aptive, while his dog is biting the captive's leg! The final scene hows Ramesses II in a pavilion, his pet lion beside him, eceiving Prince Amenhirwenemef with prisoners; a vizier and ther officials are in attendance in the lower register. Behind the avilion was originally just a stand with a tray of food on it, ut at a later date two cartouches topped with sun-disks and lumes were carved above the stand in sunk relief. The names in he cartouches were changed twice and at various times seem to ave enclosed the names of Ramesses II, Seti II, and Ramesses V.

At the west end of the forecourt are three doorways to the nner part of the temple, which was cut entirely from the rock. he two side doorways have been the subject of much iscussion over the years. It appears that they were part of the riginal plan for the temple, were later bricked up, perhaps uring the reign of a later pharaoh, and were then reopened vhen the temple was converted to a church. On both the outer nd inner sides of these two doorways traces of the later

roughly carved figures can be seen, which were partially
destroyed when the doorways were re-opened. On the outer
surfaces of the door frames the figures of Amun (by the left
doorway) and Horus (by the right doorway) can be faintly
seen on top of the original hieroglyphic inscription. Inside, an
arm holding a scimitar is faintly visible beside each doorway.

The rock-cut portion of the temple consists of a vestibule
and a sanctuary, where the reliefs and colors are well preserved.
In the vestibule (C) are two fluted proto-Doric columns, a
type also found in the Temple of Amada. The relief carvings in
fine-quality raised relief have smiting scenes on the outer walls,
Ramesses II smiting a Nubian on the south side (8) and a
Libyan on the north (12), and the king in the presence of
various deities on the other walls. In the west wall on either
side of the central doorway to the sanctuary is an unusual
feature, a small niche with statues of Ramesses II and two
deities cut from the rock. In the southern niche he appears with
Horus of Baki and Isis (10), and in the northern niche with
Khnum, the god of Elephantine, and his consort Anukis (14).
The two side doorways of the entrance may originally have
been planned to give access to each of the niches.

The central section of the ceiling between the two columns
is painted with a panel of vultures and winged cobras, Nekhbet
and Wadjet, the two patron goddesses of Upper and Lower
Egypt. The cartouches of Ramesses II are painted horizontally
between the wings of the two goddesses. The names and titles
of the king are inscribed on the columns and abaci, and his
names with prayers to the gods on the architraves.

The sanctuary (D) is also well preserved, with the exception
of the niche in the rear wall, where three seated figures
originally carved there are no longer present. They were
presumably destroyed when the temple became a church, and
none of the texts around the niche give any clue to their
identity, although they were almost certainly Ramesses II
between two gods, perhaps Amun and Horus. There are no
pictures of sacred barks on the sanctuary walls, which is rather
unusual, but the king is shown offering to an assortment of

eities, and on the right and left of the doorway on the inside he is shown as a boy being suckled by a goddess, Isis on the right and Anukis on the left (17, 18).

New Sebua

The Temple of Wadi al-Sebua *(plan 3, page 96)*

'The Temple of Ramesses-Mery-Amun in the Estate of Amun
The Arabic name for the locality where this temple stood
Wadi al-Sebua, 'Valley of the Lions,' is derived from the avenu
of sphinxes that led up to the temple. The 'drowning sphinxe
of al-Sebua were an evocative reminder during the Nubia
Rescue Campaign of what would be lost for ever withou
international cooperation. The temple dates to the reign o
Ramesses II (1279–1212 BC), and was moved to a new site abou
four kilometers west of its original position by the Egyptia
Antiquities Organization between 1961 and 1965.

The temple was built under the supervision of the vicero
of Kush, Setau, who held this post between Years 35 and 50 o
Ramesses II's reign; he was also in charge of the building o
Ramesses' temple at Gerf Hussein, which had the same plan a
Wadi al-Sebua.

The forepart of the building is free-standing, while the rea
portion is rock-cut, and the temple was dedicated to the cult
of Re-Harakhti and Amun-Re, as well as the deified pharaol
In the early centuries AD the rear part of the temple wa
converted into a Coptic church, when the reliefs were covere
with plaster painted with Christian motifs and the rock-hew
statues in the sanctuary were destroyed. However, as was th
case elsewhere, the plaster helped to preserve the earlie
decoration, which is particularly evident in this temple, wher
the carvings are in much better condition in the part of th
building that was used as a church.

The temple area is entered by a stone gateway, which was originally incorporated in a mud-brick enclosure wall. The wall could not be saved and has not been reconstructed, but its position is more or less delineated on the right and left sides of the temple by a dry-stone wall. The gateway is adorned with a colossal standing statue and a sphinx of Ramesses II on each side. These rest on high stone pedestals carved with bound prisoners, Africans on the south and Asiatics and Libyans on the north. Libyan captives were employed to build the temple, as they were also at Abu Simbel. Stelae at Abu Simbel of Setau and a military commander named Ramose record this fact.

The gateway leads to the first court (A), which has an avenue of six human-headed sphinxes wearing the double crown. The king's face wears a rather self-satisfied expression. The front of each base shows a *iunmutef* priest before the king's cartouches, and the sides have bound prisoners. Eleven stelae of Setau that stood against the north and south walls of this court are now in the Cairo Museum. As substitutes for a sacred lake, there were two rectangular stone ablution basins, one on either side of the court. They have not been replaced in their original positions but are lying together on the sand about one hundred meters to the northeast of the temple near the lake shore, opposite the custodians' hut.

At the west end of the court is another stone gateway, which was set into a brick pylon, although the brick towers have not been reconstructed, so the gateway stands alone. The upper section is partially destroyed, but the remainder is decorated with scenes of the king before various gods, a kneeling figure adoring the royal cartouches at the base on each side.

In the second court (B), beyond the gateway, the sphinx avenue continues, but here the four sphinxes are falcon-headed and represent four forms of Horus, of Maha and Miam on the left, and of Baki and Edfu on the right (4–7). There is a statuette of the king between the front paws of each sphinx. Steps lead up to the raised platform on which the temple itself stands. The entrance of the temple is through a traditional

stone pylon (C). On the left of the doorway is a standing
colossus of Ramesses II, holding a staff in his left hand, which
is adorned with the ram's head of Amun-Re. Behind the king's
left leg is a carving of his daughter Bint-Anath, who also
became his wife. The partner to this statue, which originally
stood to the right of the doorway, is now lying rather
forlornly on the sand about thirty meters north of the temple.
The fact that it is prone does, however, enable one to see the
hole in the top of the head where the double crown (which is
lying nearby) fitted on top of the king's Nubian wig. The staff
of this statue is topped with the falcon head of Re-Harakhti.
The legs of the statue are missing, which probably explains
why it has not been re-erected in its original position, but it is
to be hoped that this can be achieved sometime in the not too
distant future, as the rest of the statue is in good condition
and having both statues in place would restore the former
grandeur of the temple façade.

It is interesting to note that there are no flagpole grooves in
the towers of the entrance pylon, which is unusual. The towers
are decorated with the customary reliefs of the king smiting
captives, before Amun-Re on the left and Re-Harakhti on the
right (8, 9). Near the doorway on each side are four registers of
nome-goddesses offering to the royal cartouches (10, 11), while
the lintel and jambs show Ramesses II offering to different
gods, with more captives at the base (12). On the lintel on the
inner side of the doorway, Ramesses is shown before Re-
Harakhti and his deified self.

Inside the pylon is the open court (D) of the conventional
temple, with a colonnade right and left. The columns are
fronted by Osiris statues of the king, his hands crossed on his
chest holding the crook and flail scepters, but most of the
statues are now headless and all are rather dilapidated. The
scenes on the rear of the pylon are reasonably clear, but those
on the north and south walls are less easy to distinguish
because of weathering and because of the coarse nature of the
sandstone blocks with which the walls were constructed.
Standardized offering scenes comprise the major part, with a

procession of some of the numerous royal children below the main scenes on every wall, a total of fifty-four princesses and fifty-three princes.

At the far end of the court, steps with ramps lead up to a narrow terrace with royal titles carved along the edge. Here is the entrance to the pillared hall (E), with a small damaged sphinx on each side. Enough of the left-hand one remains, however, to show that it had the head of a falcon; the other one, now headless, may have had the ram's head of Amun-Re. On the façade, the deified Ramesses II again appears in the company of other gods. Scenes on the lintels, jambs, and passageway of the doorway are similar to those in the pylon entrance (19).

The rest of the temple is cut from the rock, and it was this section that was converted into a Christian church. The original entrance was bricked up to create a double doorway with arches, which was still in place before the temple was moved, but was taken down during its dismantling. The hypostyle hall that follows has twelve square pillars. Those on each side of the central aisle were originally Osirid, but the figures of the king were chiseled away when the hall became part of the church. The walls are covered with large-scale scenes of the king with various deities, and some traces of color survive, particularly in a scene of Ramesses II offering libation and incense to Onuris-Shu, Tefnut, and Nekhbet in the northeast corner (23). Areas of color like this are a good indication of the original appearance of the wall reliefs.

The doorway at the west end gives access to a transverse vestibule (F) preceding the sanctuary. These inner rooms are the best preserved in the temple, both as regards the carving and in the amount of color preserved. Among the scenes of Ramesses II with the gods is an unusual depiction of Hathor with a woman's body and a cow's head instead of a human one, surmounted by her usual cow's horns and sun-disk headdress (east wall, 29). The four Nubian Horuses also feature, as well as major gods of the Egyptian pantheon. To the left and right of the vestibule is a long, narrow side-room, probably used as a storeroom. Both these rooms are also decorated with carved scenes in a good state of preservation.

Along the west side of the vestibule are three smaller chambers, the sanctuary (G) in the center flanked by two side chapels, all again with colorful decoration. As one would expect, the left and right walls of the sanctuary depict the king before the sacred barks of Amun-Re (34) and Re-Harakhti (35). The niche in the west wall (36) was carved with statues of Amun-Re, Re-Harakhti, and Ramesses II as a god, but these were destroyed during the Christian conversion. The pharaonic carvings were covered with plaster painted with Christian figures, but since most of this plaster has now disappeared revealing the earlier scenes underneath, the preservation of a large portion of Christian plaster in the sanctuary-niche has resulted in the somewhat incongruous picture of Ramesses II offering flowers to St. Peter! Only the upper part of the painted figure of the saint now survives, but his head with a halo and the top of a large key, which he is holding in his left hand, can still be distinguished.

On the exterior of the temple some reliefs are still visible on the north outer wall of the pillared hall (41), which was once the south wall of a corridor formed between this wall and the mud-brick enclosure wall.

In the area between the Temple of Wadi al-Sebua and those of Dakka and Maharraqa about one kilometer to the north, is a high rocky outcrop where a number of 'caves' are being prepared to house the carvings from several rock-cut shrines from the lower parts of the headland of Qasr Ibrim. One of these shrines, belonging to Usersatet, viceroy of Kush under Amenophis II of the Eighteenth Dynasty (1453–1419 BC), has been reconstructed in the new Nubia Museum in Aswan. Lying on the sand nearby are various inscribed blocks, some from the Chapel of Horemheb at Abu Oda south of Abu Simbel, as well as some prehistoric petroglyphs.

The Temple of Dakka *(plan 4, page 100)*

'The Temple of Thoth of Pnubs'

he Temple of Dakka with its elegant pylon stood forty
ilometers north of its present site and was dismantled and
reconstructed at New Sebua by the Egyptian Antiquities
Organization between 1961 and 1965. The temple was started
by the Meroitic king Arkamani (known in Greek as
Ergamenes), and was added to by his contemporary, Ptolemy
V of Egypt (222–205 BC), with decoration by later Ptolemies.
n the Roman Period a pylon and sanctuary were also added.
There is a possibility that there was an earlier temple on the
ite, as reports on the temple before it was moved mention
blocks in the pavement with the cartouche of Tuthmosis III,
but these may have come from the nearby fortress of Quban.

Although the Greek name for the town of Dakka was
Pselkis, meaning 'the scorpion,' the temple was dedicated to a
ocal form of Thoth, the god of wisdom, known as Thoth of
Pnubs (Pnubs means 'the sycamore-fig tree'), with the goddess
Tefnut as his consort, particularly in her lioness aspect, and
Arsenuphis as the third member of the triad, or holy family.
n the creation myth associated with the sun god Atum,
Tefnut is the goddess of moisture and twin-sister of Shu, the
god of air. However, she is also the 'eye of the sun god Re,'
and in this role features in an interesting myth concerning
Nubia. Angry with her father, Tefnut went to Nubia, where
he took on the form of a raging lioness and terrorized the
and. Re sent Thoth and Shu to persuade her to come back to
Egypt, which they eventually managed to do. This is similar to
a myth about Hathor, another daughter of the sun god, who
also personified the eye of Re and went on the rampage in
Nubia. Arsenuphis was a Nubian god of the Meroitic Period
identified with Shu. The Egyptian form of his name was
Iryhemesnefer, which means 'the good companion.' In the
Temple of Dakka, Thoth of Pnubs is often shown in human
orm wearing the short Nubian wig with a headdress of four
eathers, and Arsenuphis sometimes also appears in this form,

the accompanying hieroglyphic inscription being the only means of identification in these instances.

The temple follows the traditional plan, with entrance pylon, open court, pronaos, and sanctuary, although the side walls of the open court (B) beyond the pylon have now disappeared, as has also the outer enclosure wall of the temple. The temple is oriented north–south, as it was in its original position, where it was parallel to the Nile, and it has also been resited on rising ground. The quality of relief carving in this small temple varies quite considerably from the fine, raised relief of the early parts of the building, to the rough, rather crude relief of the Roman sanctuary.

The imposing pylon (A), which at over twelve meters in height seems to dwarf the rest of the building, has scenes in carved relief on the left-hand side of the entrance passage, and the winged sun-disk is carved above the doorway. Except for the two vertical grooves for flagpoles in front, the towers of the pylon are largely unadorned, although rough sketches of Horus and other figures can be seen here and there on the jambs and the inner faces of the towers. Meroitic graffiti can also be seen, particularly among the relief carving in the entrance passage (2), where the early form of cursive Meroitic script suggests that this graffito was carved about 23 BC, during the retreat of the Meroites after their attack on Aswan under Queen Amanirenas. Each tower of the pylon has an internal staircase, which leads up to the roof and provides access to a large room on each of three stories, possibly used as storerooms. From the top of the pylon there is a commanding view of the lake, the small Roman temple of Maharraqa nearby to the east between Dakka and the lake shore, and the Ramesside temple of Wadi al-Sebua about one kilometer to the south.

In many of the scenes throughout the temple the king who is performing the rituals is not specifically named, but is simply identified by the title 'Pharaoh,' (*per-aa*, literally 'Great House'), written in a cartouche. However, cartouches with the names of Arkamani, Ptolemies IV, VI, VII, and VIII, and the

Roman emperors Augustus and Tiberius indicate where work was carried out during their reigns.

The decoration of the outer face of the pronaos and the entrance passage was carried out under Ptolemy VII, as he and his queen, Cleopatra III, are shown in scenes on the side walls in the company of various gods (6–8). On the columns themselves are inscriptions mentioning Ptolemies II to VII. The original screen-walls had disappeared before the temple was moved, so they have been replaced by modern stonework to fill the spaces between the columns. Inside the pronaos (C), the rear of the façade, which is now destroyed, formerly depicted Augustus on the two screen-walls, according to Champollion's description of the temple during his visit in 1828–29. With the Egyptians' love of symmetry in art, scenes on one wall are often complemented by similar scenes at the same location on the opposite wall. Thus we find here that a representation of Augustus occurs on the south wall to the left of the doorway (13). The the scenes on the east wall of the pronaos are arranged in three registers and show Pharaoh offering to different gods and goddesses, in a style characteristic of the Ptolemaic Period (compare these with the scenes in the Temple of Kalabsha, for example). The deities include Thoth of Pnubs, Tefnut, Amun, Osiris, Isis, Horus, Re-Harakhti, Hathor, Shu, and Ptah, and one can easily recognize the triad of Abydos (Osiris, Isis, and Horus) in the middle register (12). The scenes on the west wall and most of the south wall are now largely destroyed. The king's name is given in the cartouches simply as 'Pharaoh' in each case. The raised relief carving here is generally of good quality and the ceiling is decorated with alternating vultures and winged cobras, the patron goddesses of Upper and Lower Egypt, Nekhbet and Wadjet.

The doorway (16) to the next section of the temple, the vestibule (D), has on the lintel a double scene of Ptolemy IV with Queen Arsinoe III offering the Maat figure to Thoth of Pnubs and Wepset on the left, and to other gods, now lost, on the right. The jambs show the pharaoh offering to Re-Harakhti, Khnum-Re, and Hathor in separate scenes on the

left, and to Amun-Re, Horus, and Isis on the right, with a
Nile god at the base on each side. The inner side of the
doorway has similar decoration, the lintel showing Isis giving
life to the cartouches of Ptolemy IV and his wife Arsinoe III;
his grandfather Ptolemy II and his wife Arsinoe II; and his
father Ptolemy III and his wife Berenice II. The jambs show
Pharaoh offering to the goddesses Satis, Isis, Anukis, and
Hathor, again with Nile gods at the base.

The next part is the chapel of Arkamani (E), the Meroitic
king, whose name appears on the architrave above the door
(19). This was the sanctuary of the temple before the addition
of the Roman sanctuary beyond. On the lintel is a double scene
showing the Roman emperor Tiberius followed by a Queen
Cleopatra, offering the Maat figure to Thoth and Wepset on
the left, and to Osiris and Isis on the right. The jambs depict
Pharaoh and various deities. Inside this chapel all four walls are
divided into three registers, with the king offering to an
assortment of gods and goddesses. The raised relief is again well
executed. The deified Imhotep, the chief minister and architect
of King Djoser of the Third Dynasty, can be seen on the north
wall, left side, second register (22), while a figure described as
Pharaoh of Senmet (the island of Bigeh near Philae, where there
was a shrine to Osiris) is depicted on the west wall, left end,
second register (24). The same figure is also shown in the
corresponding position on the opposite (east) wall (23). As
well as the triad of the temple (Thoth, Tefnut, and
Arsenuphis), the most frequently occurring deities are Osiris,
Isis, Horus, and Hathor. At the base of the walls are Nile gods
and field goddesses, and at the top is an elaborate frieze with
the cartouches of Arkamani, ibises on shrines, and falcons. On
the south wall, on the left side of the doorway to the
sanctuary (25), is a scene showing the king offering wine to
Isis, with an inscription in four and a half vertical columns
stating that Isis has given him the Land of 'Ta-kens,' or Lower
Nubia, from Aswan to Takhampso (the island of Derar near
Maharraqa), that is the Dodekaschoinos. During the Roman
Period a narrow chapel was cut in the thickness of the east wall

27). Well-preserved scenes of Pharaoh and gods occur on the right and left walls, while the rear wall has an interesting depiction of Thoth as an ape adoring Tefnut, who is shown as a lioness. Thoth disguised himself as a baboon when he went to Nubia to look for her. Above this scene are two ibises on pedestals decorated with crouching lions (the ibis was another manifestation of Thoth), while below are falcons protecting Pharaoh's cartouches, and two more lions, which may represent Shu and Tefnut, the twin children of Atum, who were worshiped elsewhere in Egypt as a pair of lions. A staircase in the thickness of the west wall leads up onto the roof of the temple and also gives access to a crypt.

The chamber at the rear of the temple is the Roman sanctuary (F), where the relief is crudely carved, in contrast to the precise work of the preceding chamber. Normal custom was for the carving inside the temple to be done in raised relief (where the background is cut away), sunk relief being reserved for exterior walls, but here on the north wall of the Roman sanctuary (30, 31) the decoration is in sunk relief, perhaps because this was originally the outer, rear wall of the temple before the addition of the sanctuary. The scenes on all four walls are arranged across two registers. Here also the cartouches contain only the title 'Pharaoh.' On the north wall, on each side of the doorway, Pharaoh offers to the four Nubian forms of Horus, two on each side, of Baki and Buhen on the right and of Miam and Maha on the left. Other scenes show Pharaoh with deities familiar from other parts of the temple, including Thoth, Tefnut, Shu, Osiris, Isis, and Horus. A frieze along the tops of the walls shows the cartouches of Pharaoh protected by falcons. At the base of the walls is a procession of Nile gods with offerings. At the bottom of the west side of the north wall (31) is a depiction of Thoth as an ape under the sacred sycamore tree, over which a Nile god is pouring water. Above this scene, on the same wall, is a scene of the king before Isis and Horus. Between the heads of the king and goddess, underneath the hieroglyphic inscription, is a two-line graffito in Egyptian demotic, one of many throughout the temple.

This one was written by the Roman governor Selewe, and commemorates the building of the sanctuary in Year 40 of Emperor Augustus (AD 10). Two pieces of pink granite, the top and bottom of a naos, or shrine, have been somewhat roughly reconstructed toward the rear of the sanctuary.

There is a small amount of decoration on the exterior walls of the temple. On the west wall (35, 36) are carvings of Horus, Thoth, Arsenuphis, Tefnut, and Hathor, while high up on the east wall to the left of the side doorway (37), is a somewhat comical carving of a lion's head, a simplified form of the gargoyle waterspout for draining water off the roof.

The Temple of Maharraqa

Temple of Serapis

The small Roman Temple of Maharraqa was originally sited fifty kilometers north of its present position, near the village of Ofendina, site of the ancient town of Hierasykaminos, 'the place of the sacred sycamore-fig tree,' which was the southern frontier of Egypt in Greco-Roman times. The temple was moved to New Sebua by the Egyptian Antiquities Organization in 1961.

The decoration of the temple was never completed, floral column capitals remaining unfinished, and although the temple is usually described as being dedicated to Serapis, the few relief carvings that survive, some from this temple and a few more from a smaller structure that stood closer to the Nile, actually depict Osiris, Isis, Horus, Thoth, and Tefnut.

The temple consists of one hall with a colonnade of six columns on the north side, three on the west side, and six joined by screen-walls on the south side, with a doorway in the center to a narrow chamber. On the east wall of this chamber, a piece of broken relief carving has been inserted in the reconstructed wall. It is part of a scene showing a king offering to Osiris and Isis. What appear to be figures of a king and some gods can be seen roughly sketched in reddish-brown paint in various places on the south wall. At the northeast angle of the main hall of the temple is a spiral staircase going up to the roof, the only spiral staircase known in an ancient Egyptian building.

There is evidence that the temple of Maharraqa was later used as a Christian church. Some vaulting is preserved over the east door, where the original entrance of the temple was closed up and plastered over to form an apse (sanctuary-niche) at the east end of the church, and a 'new' door was made in the west wall.

Each evening after dinner on the Lake Nasser cruises the three temples at New Sebua are floodlit for about half an hour, making a romantic tableau against the velvet sky with myriads of stars, which are normally obliterated for most of us by modern street-lighting. At night on Lake Nasser, stargazers will be well rewarded; the Southern Cross is visible at certain times of the year, for example. Seeing the constellations stretching across from one watery horizon to the other, one can understand how the ancient Egyptians envisaged the star-studded body of the sky-goddess Nut arched across the earth.

New Amada

The Temple of Amada *(plan 5, page 104)*

'The Temple of Re-Harakhti'

Situated in one of the most dramatically beautiful parts of
Nubia, the Temple of Amada is the oldest surviving
monument on Lake Nasser and also one of the most delightful.
The Nile made a large bend at this point and flowed due south
for several kilometers. Consequently, as the lake follows
approximately the same course, the left bank is now on the east
instead of the west. Although the exterior of the temple is very
plain, the interior contains some of the finest relief carving to
be seen in any of the Nubian monuments. It was built by the
kings Tuthmosis III, Amenophis II, and Tuthmosis IV (1504–
1386 BC) of the Eighteenth Dynasty, and restoration and
further decoration were carried out by the kings of the
Nineteenth Dynasty. During the reign of Akhenaten (1350–
1334 BC), with his monotheistic cult of the Aten, the name of
Amun was erased throughout the temple; it was later restored
under Seti I (1291–1278 BC). In the early Christian period the
temple was converted into a church, a mud-brick dome was
built on the roof, and the brightly colored relief carvings were
covered with a layer of plaster. Fortunately this was beneficial
rather than detrimental to the reliefs in the long run, as the
plaster protected both the reliefs and the colors.

Apart from the excellence of its decoration and its value as
an example of New Kingdom architecture, the Temple of
Amada contains two important historical inscriptions. The

first is in the sanctuary of the temple (31) and describes the completion and dedication of the temple by Amenophis II, concluding with an account of a military campaign against the Asiatics in the second year of that king's reign, in which he dealt particularly ruthlessly with seven important prisoners-of-war. The other inscription, on the left of the entrance doorway, records the suppression of a Libyan-backed rebellion in Nubia in Year 4 of Merenptah, the successor of Ramesses II (3).

During the Nubian Rescue Campaign, the Temple of Amada was moved by a team of French engineers. After the forepart of the temple was dismantled, the rear section was jacked up onto flatcars and gradually moved backward on rail track for 2.6 kilometers, to a position beyond the highest limit predicted for the High Dam lake. This painstaking maneuver, which was a race against time as the water was already rising, took just three months and was a prodigious feat of engineering.

The temple was dedicated to the gods Amun-Re and Re-Harakhti, as were most of the temples in Nubia. At the entrance of the temple is a small pylon gateway (A), with a stone doorway flanked by side wings of sun-dried mud brick. Most of the original mud brick had disappeared by the mid-nineteenth century, but when the temple was moved to its new location, the two wings were partially reconstructed to give an indication of their original appearance. The relief carving on the doorway, which is very shallow, shows Tuthmosis III with Re-Harakhti on the right (1) and Amenophis II with the same god on the left (2). On the left of the doorway passage (3), beneath a scene showing Amenophis II before Re-Harakhti and Montu, is the inscription of Merenptah; on the right (4) is a representation of Setau, viceroy of Nubia during the reign of Ramesses II, who was responsible for the building of the Temple of Wadi al-Sebua. Throughout the temple are small scenes that were added later showing various viceroys of Kush (Setau, Hekanakht, and Messuy), from the reigns of Ramesses II and Merenptah, and the chancellor Bay from the time of Siptah, Merenptah's successor.

The construction of the temple, from sandstone blocks quarried in the vicinity, was begun by Tuthmosis III (1504–1450 BC) and completed by his son Amenophis II (1453–1410 BC). At the time, the entrance through the pylon led into an open court enclosed by mud-brick walls and the temple proper was fronted by a portico of four proto-Doric columns (so called because they predate the Greek fluted columns of that design). Tuthmosis IV (1419–1386 BC) converted the open court into a roofed pillared hall by erecting twelve square pillars in three rows, with connecting walls between the lateral pillars.

The pillars and side walls of the pillared hall (B) are decorated with scenes of Tuthmosis IV in the company of various gods and goddesses, while scenes on the right and left of the doorway into the temple proper depict Tuthmosis III and Amenophis II. On the left side of the hall (7), an inscription describes Tuthmosis IV as "beloved of Senusert III," the Twelfth Dynasty pharaoh who was regarded as a god in Nubian monuments of the New Kingdom for his conquest of Nubia. The crude carvings of camels on the cornice of the temple façade are not contemporary with the pharaonic decoration, but are graffiti that were probably made by travelers or Bedouin in the early Middle Ages, when the building was no longer used as a church and was partly filled with sand. Amelia Edwards, the British writer and Egyptophile, who visited Amada in 1873, mentions in her book *A Thousand Miles Up the Nile* that the temple was "half-choked" with sand, so that she and her fellow travelers had to crawl into the sanctuary on their hands and knees. The sand had drifted so high at the back of the temple that it was possible to climb up onto the roof with ease.

Beyond the portico (C), the inner part of the temple consists of a vestibule and the sanctuary, which is flanked by a side chamber and small cult chamber on each side. The relief carvings and their colors are best preserved in this part of the temple and compare with the finest of Eighteenth Dynasty reliefs. The kings portrayed are Tuthmosis III and Amenophis

The Temple of Dendur, Metropolitan Museum, New York.

The pronaos in the Temple of Kalabsha, New Kalabsha

The Kiosk of Qertassi, New Kalabsha.

The forecourt of the Temple of Beit al-Wali, New Kalabsha.

The Avenue of Sphinxes, Wadi al-Sebua, New Sebua.

The Temple of Dakka, New Sebua.

The Temple of Maharraqa, New Sebua.

The Temple of Amada, New Amada.

The Temple of Derr, New Amada.

Offering scene in the Tomb of Pennut (rear wall, right side), New Amada.

Qasr Ibrim.

The Great Temple, Abu Simbel.

The great pillared hall of the Great Temple, Abu Simbel.

The sanctuary of the Great Temple, Abu Simbel.

Ramesses II crowned by Seth of Nubet and Horus of Maha, Small Temple, Abu Simbel.

I. In the vestibule (D) on the left-hand side are coronation scenes, with Amenophis II being ritually purified by Thoth and Horus (22) and performing a ritual run with an oar and a *hap* instrument (23), while on the right-hand side both kings appear in the presence of different deities. On either side of the doorway to the sanctuary are parallel scenes of the two kings being embraced by one of the gods of the temple, Amenophis II by Re-Harakhti on the left (24), and Tuthmosis III by Amun-Re on the right (27).

In the sanctuary (E) the side walls show the respective kings in complementary scenes with several deities, while the rear wall (31) is entirely taken up by the inscription from Year 3 of Amenophis II, surmounted by a scene of the same king in a boat offering wine to Re-Harakhti and Amun-Re. The inscription refers to the king's campaigns in Syria and his ruthless treatment of the bodies of seven Syrian chieftains, whom he had clubbed to death. The bodies were brought back to Egypt hanging at the prow of the king's own ship; six of them were displayed on the walls of Thebes, and the seventh was taken south to Napata in Upper Nubia, where it received similar treatment. The new king wished, as he goes on to say, to make it emphatically clear to his subjects, particularly those in the far corners of his empire, that he was as capable a ruler as his eminent predecessor, and would brook no insurrection or challenge to his authority.

Scenes in the two small cult chambers (F) and the left-side room are predominantly offering scenes, with either Tuthmosis III or Amenophis II offering different items to various gods. The scenes in the right-hand side room (G 39, 40), however, are more interesting, as they are concerned with the ceremonial foundation and consecration of the temple. The official foundation of a temple consisted of a series of ceremonies, which formally delineated the position and area of the temple and included the 'stretching of the cord,' running a ritual course, the making and laying of bricks, and the official dedication, or 'handing over,' of a temple to its god. During the consecration, animals were slaughtered and offered to the

gods of the temple, and vestments and ritual implements wer
also consecrated.

The outer walls of Amada Temple are undecorated apar
from two Ramesside graffiti on the rear wall (42), and tw
depictions of Viceroy Messuy on the south wall (43).

The Temple of Derr *(plan 6, page 108)*

'The Temple of Ramesses-Mery-Amun in the Estate of Re'
This temple of Ramesses II, which is partially rock-cut, wa
originally situated on the opposite bank of the Nile and eleve
kilometers further southwest. It was, in fact, the onl
pharaonic temple on the east bank in Nubia—al-Lesiya, whic
was also on the east bank and dates to the reign of Tuthmos
III, being only a small rock-cut shrine (see below). The templ
is somewhat crude in construction and decoration, the muc
weathered and damaged forepart of the building making thi
the first impression for the visitor. However, well-preserve
scenes in the pillared hall have a lively vigor, reminiscent of th
scenes at Abu Simbel. As at the latter temple, Ramesses II wa
worshiped in the Temple of Derr as a living god, and is show
offering to his deified self.

The temple was dismantled by a team of Egyptia
archaeologists during the Nubian Rescue Campaign and wa
reconstructed close to the Temple of Amada. Amelia Edward
described it in 1873 as an ugly ruin with no charm, an
certainly it can hardly be described as picturesque, but th
unattractive exterior is redeemed by the well-preserved carve
reliefs inside, which owe their preservation to the fact that, lik
the Temple of Amada, Derr was also later used as a Christia
church, when the pharaonic carvings were covered with plaster.

The temple was originally fronted by a gateway and hall c
square pillars, but no traces of the gateway now survive and th
pillars stand only up to a height of about 1.25 meters. Th
walls and pillars of this first pillared hall (A) were probabl
rock-hewn and masonry seems to have been used for roofin

as grooves cut in the architraves above the Osirid pillars of the entrance portico may have been for the ends of stone beams. The side walls were decorated with scenes of Ramesses II's military campaigns in Nubia, similar to scenes in his Beit al-Wali temple, but they are now virtually destroyed. A thick coating of bird droppings covers the exterior of the temple, and adds to the difficulty of trying to distinguish traces of the carved figures. Part of the king's chariot and the bellies and legs of the two horses pulling it are visible on the left wall.

The entrance to the main part of the temple has a portico of four square pillars fronted by colossal statues of Ramesses II. The statues survive in rough only up to the waist and the upper part is lost in each case. The walls flanking the doorway have traditional scenes of the king smiting the enemies of Egypt, before Re-Harakhti on the left (3), and before Amun-Re on the right (7). In each case he is followed by his *ka* and accompanied by his pet lion, while below each scene is a procession of some of the royal children, eight princes on the left and nine princesses on the right.

The interior of the temple, all of which was cut out of the rock, comprises a hall with six pillars, followed by the sanctuary, which has a side chamber on each side. In general the hewing of the temple was very roughly executed, with "no straight lines or right-angles anywhere," according to Blackman, who examined and published the temple in 1913. The sculpture was also poor, being only roughly cut in stone, then finished in stucco with painted details. In the second pillared hall (B) the pillars show Ramesses II with various gods, while the side walls depict the sacred model boat of Re-Harakhti being carried in procession on the shoulders of priests (10, 14). The king appears twice in the same scene, walking beside the sacred boat wearing the leopard skin in his role as high priest, and burning incense before the sacred boat. On the left wall the king then offers to Amun-Kamutef, the fertility god (11), while on the right wall he receives the symbol of jubilee from Amun-Re and Mut, in the company of Thoth, Montu, and Harsiesi (15). On the ceiling of the central aisle faint traces of the original painted stucco of vultures with wings outspread alternating with the cartouches of Ramesses II can still be seen.

At the rear of this second pillared hall are three chambers, the middle one of which is the sanctuary of the temple. On either side of the doorway leading to the sanctuary the king offers to different gods, including (on the right of the door) his deified self in the company of Amun-Re and Mut (17). The carved doorway to the sanctuary has scenes of the king performing two versions of the 'ritual run' on the lintel and three registers on each jamb showing Ramesses II before a different deity in each. In the thickness of the doorway the king receives the symbol of life from Amun-Re on the left, and from Re-Harakhti on the right. Inside the sanctuary (C) a certain amount of color is preserved. On each side of the doorway the king appears with a libation vase (19, 20). The scenes on the right and left walls are very similar. On both sides the king burns incense and pours a libation before the sacred bark of Re-Harakhti, which rests on a stand. On the left wall Ramesses then offers cloth to Ptah (21), while on the right wall (22) he anoints Re-Harakhti, very delicately, with his little finger! At the back of this chamber four statues were originally carved in the solid rock. They represented (from left to right) Ptah, Amun-Re, the deified Ramesses II, and Re-Harakhti, the same gods carved in the sanctuary at Abu Simbel. However, the statues were hacked out when the temple was converted into a church in the early Christian period. Flanking the sanctuary are side-chambers (D, E), which were probably used as storerooms. Both chambers are decorated with carved reliefs of the king offering to various gods, and the room on the left (D) has a low shelf cut out of the rock.

The Tomb of Pennut *(plan 7, page 111)*

After rather a surfeit of temples, the delightful little tomb of Pennut (sometimes transliterated from the hieroglyphs as

Penne), comes as a welcome change. It is a small rock-cut tomb belonging to a high official from the time of Ramesses VI (1141–1133 BC) and was moved during the UNESCO Campaign from its original location at Aniba, forty kilometers to the south of its present site at New Amada, five to ten minutes' walk south of the reconstructed Temple of Derr. Unfortunately, the relief carvings from the tomb have been greatly damaged over the past sixty years, as the publication of the tomb by Steindorff in 1937 shows that the carvings were then virtually intact, whereas only about half of them now survive in situ. However, enough is visible to impress the viewer, with even some traces of color.

The inscriptions name Pennut as Deputy of Wawat, Chief of the Quarry-Service, and Steward of Horus, Lord of Miam (the ancient name for Aniba), identifying him as the chief administrator in Lower Nubia under the viceroy of Kush. It is not clear from the inscriptions, or the depictions of Pennut in his tomb, whether he was a native Egyptian or an Egyptianized Nubian. Egyptians usually made certain that they were buried in their homeland, even if they died abroad, whereas not only was Pennut buried at Aniba but several members of his family, some of whom had prominent positions in the administration of Wawat (Lower Nubia), had tombs there as well. Pennut's tomb follows the usual pattern of a rock-cut tomb of the New Kingdom, with a small offering-chapel decorated with carved and painted scenes in sunk relief. Those on the left side of the tomb depict religious subjects particularly associated with the judgment of the dead and the afterlife (2–4), while those on the right side show events and personalities from Pennut's life (5–7). At the rear of the chapel is a small niche with three statues hewn out of the rock. The undecorated burial chamber was below the floor of the offering-chapel.

One of the most significant events in Pennut's life was his dedication of a statue of King Ramesses VI to the temple at Miam, presumably that of Horus, of which Pennut was a steward, and the endowment of land to maintain it. Pennut was rewarded by the king with a gift of two silver vases, an

episode that is recorded on the wall to the right of the
doorway as one enters the tomb (5), and on the long right-
hand wall (6). This wall originally had a series of scenes
connected with Pennut's dedication of the king's statue,
starting with a portrayal of Ramesses VI at the top left
addressing the viceroy of Kush about Pennut's reward, then a
scene of the viceroy and another official adoring the statue of
the king. Sadly almost all of the relief carvings on this wall have
been cut away, except for a small part at the right, where one
can see at the top Pennut being dressed for this special occasion
by two servants, and at the bottom some of his daughters.

The left side of the tomb has not fared so badly, except for
the lower portion of the wall to the left of the entrance, where
the scenes of Pennut's funeral procession and the Weighing of
the Heart have disappeared. In the doorway itself, on the left
side, is a well-preserved depiction of Pennut and his wife
Takha, a priestess in the Temple of Horus at Miam (1).

Above the doorway to the niche at the back of the tomb is
the sun-disk in a boat, with an adoring baboon on either side
(8). The niche originally contained three unfinished statues, the
middle one apparently cow-headed, from which one would
assume that the statues represented Pennut and his wife on
either side of the Hathor cow, goddess of the Western
Mountain, the way to the next life.

Qasr Ibrim

Qasr Ibrim was situated on the highest of three headlands located on the east side of the Nile about sixty kilometers north of Abu Simbel, until the building of the Aswan High Dam and the creation of Lake Nasser, which submerged the other headlands to north and south, and by 1975 turned Qasr Ibrim into an island. It is, however, the only archaeological site in Egyptian Nubia that is still above the water, and the Egypt Exploration Society continues to excavate here every two years. Ibrim has provided a great deal of information about the history of Lower Nubia and its relations with Egyptians, Romans, Meroites, and others over its three thousand years of occupation. Because of the fragile nature of the ruins and artifacts that cover every inch of the site, it is not permitted for visitors to disembark and actually walk around it. Cruise ships stop beside the island for twenty to thirty minutes on their way to and from Abu Simbel, so that passengers can view the ruins from the deck. Exceptionally high floods in recent years have unfortunately submerged several more meters of the site, and have also brought viewers closer to the ruins of the church, which crowns the summit of the island. Even seeing David Roberts' painting of Ibrim made in 1838 and photographs taken before 1960, it is still difficult to imagine that this shrinking island site once stood on top of a towering headland, seventy meters high, most of which is now under water.

The Arabic name Qasr Ibrim, 'the castle of Ibrim,' is derived from the ancient Meroitic name Pedeme, which became Primis in classical texts, Phrim in medieval Coptic, and Ibrim in the late Middle Ages, with the more recent addition of Qasr, meaning 'castle.'

The earliest document found at Ibrim is a stela dated to the eighth year of Amenophis I (1543 BC), now in the British Museum, which was found reused in one of the crypts of the cathedral church that crowns the island, but the earliest major building on top of the headland is a mud-brick temple from the time of Taharka, the Nubian king of Egypt of the Twenty-fifth Dynasty (690–664 BC). There is evidence for fortifications on the site going back to about 1000 BC, but it is also possible that a fortress was built at this strategic spot during the Middle Kingdom about eight hundred years earlier, when Egypt annexed Nubia and a line of mud-brick forts was constructed along the Nile to maintain Egyptian control. The place was clearly considered important in the New Kingdom (1570–1070 BC), when four shrines were cut into the rock on the west face of the cliffs at the water's edge. The fact that Ibrim was opposite the district capital Miam (Aniba) on the west bank of the Nile, may account for this. The shrines were dedicated to the Nubian forms of Horus (especially to Horus of Miam), with other deities depicted, such as Khnum, Satis, and Hathor. Each shrine had a niche with statues of the king of the time between two gods. The best of these shrines, that of Usersatet, viceroy of Kush in the time of Amenophis II of the Eighteenth Dynasty (1453–1419 BC), has been reconstructed in the new Nubia Museum at Aswan. Others are awaiting the completion of modern rock-cut caves at New Sebua. On the headland to the south of Ibrim a stela of Seti I with the viceroy of Kush, Amenemope, was carved in the rock; this was cut away from the rock face in four pieces during the UNESCO campaign and is now at New Kalabsha just to the south of Kalabsha Temple.

In about 680 BC Taharka built a mud-brick temple on the southwestern side of the headland, which was to remain in use as a place of worship for over two thousand years, as it was later converted to a Christian church. During the late Ptolemaic Period, in the second or first century BC, the first proper fortification wall was built. More details are known of the history of Ibrim from the Roman Period onward, when it seems to have been the last outpost for the worship of the ancient gods during the spread of Christianity, and then over a thousand years later remained a stronghold of Christianity for several centuries against the rising tide of Islam.

The historical role of Ibrim seesawed between that of a military stronghold and a religious center, through the latter part of the pharaonic period and the early Christian era. The first historical reference to Ibrim, under the name Primis, is by the Greek historian Strabo, in his account of events at Aswan in 23 BC. Taking advantage of a weakening in Roman authority, the Meroitic queen Kandake and her army attacked and occupied Aswan, Elephantine, and Philae. (Kandake was the Meroitic word for 'queen,' and this particular one. was probably Queen Amanirenas.) The Nubians were expelled from Aswan and pursued into Nubia by the Roman prefect Gaius Petronius and his forces and, after being routed at Dakka, they took refuge in Ibrim for a short time. Ibrim was occupied by a Roman garrison for the next two years, and an attempt was made by the Romans to fix the southern frontier of Egypt at this point. During their occupation the Romans built a temple and a podium on the west side of the headland similar to that at Kalabsha. In 21 BC, after a further attack on Ibrim by the Nubians, a peace treaty was agreed between the Roman emperor, Augustus, and the Meroites, the Roman troops withdrew, and the frontier was established further north at Maharraqa.

Once peace had been made with Rome, Ibrim flourished. The Taharka temple was rebuilt and several new temples were constructed, so the settlement became more a religious center than a military one, with as many as six temples within the five acres of the site. Healing cults were also apparently practiced here, as happened in temples of this period in Egypt itself, for example at Kalabsha, Edfu, and Dendera. At the same time Ibrim became a major commercial center, coinciding with the general repopulation of Lower Nubia, perhaps due to the introduction of the ox-driven water-wheel. New settlers came from the north and west of the Kushite empire and may have brought with them an early version of the Nubian language that is still spoken today.

Ibrim was little effected by the collapse of the Meroitic kingdom in the mid-fourth century AD. During the Ballana Period, Ibrim continued to prosper. The inhabitants occupied stone-built houses, and there were a number of local industries in wood, leather, pottery, and cotton textiles. Wine and luxury goods were imported from Egypt. From time to time the Blemmye and Nobatae tribes from the eastern and western deserts vied for possession of Ibrim, but their activities had little effect on the commercial situation. A mud-brick temple to Isis was founded and the other Meroitic temples continued in use. In AD 390 the Roman emperor Theodosius I declared Christianity compulsory in Egypt, which resulted in the closure of pagan temples, with the exception of the Temple of Isis at Philae, where both the Blemmyes and the Nobatae worshiped. In 453 the Blemmyes reached an agreement with the Roman authorities to keep the peace in exchange for permission to worship at Philae and to borrow the statue of Isis from the temple for oracles. Paganism continued to flourish at Ibrim, and yet another temple may have been built there at this time. In about 536 Philae was forcibly closed under the orders of Justinian and part of the temple was later converted into a church.

At about the same time, Ibrim was converted to Christianity (more than two centuries after Egypt), although there are indications that there was some overlap between paganism and the new religion. The Taharka temple was converted into a church, the Isis temple was destroyed. In the seventh century the cathedral church of the Virgin Mary was built on the highest point of the headland, with some reused blocks from the earlier temples. A large terrace was made between the churches, which served as a gathering place for pilgrims, as Ibrim became a center of pilgrimage and a bishopric. Many secular houses on the headland were demolished and in the early Middle Ages a lower town-site was constructed beside the Nile, so there were fewer houses within the fortified walls.

Soon after the Arab conquest of Egypt in 640, a treaty was made between the Muslims and Christian Nubia, which maintained peace between them until 1172–73 when Ibrim was raided by Turan Shah, the brother of Saladin. As a result, the old Greco-Roman fortification walls were rebuilt and raised, and there were more houses again on the mountain-top. However, relations between the Nubians and the later Ayyubid rulers of Egypt were generally good. From the eleventh century onward, Ibrim became the headquarters of the 'eparch,' the Nubian king's governor of Lower Nubia. Conflicts between the Nubians and the Mamluks in the thirteenth and fourteenth centuries, and the ensuing political unrest, also seem to have made little difference to life at Ibrim, which continued as the principal Christian center in Lower Nubia, although its defensive walls were kept in good repair. In the fifteenth century, with the gradual break-up of the Nubian kingdoms and increased invasions by Muslim Arab nomads, Ibrim on its rocky hilltop became more and more isolated as many inhabitants of Lower Nubia moved further south for safety, and those who remained converted to Islam.

In 1517 Egypt was conquered by the Ottoman Turks, and soon afterward Lower Nubia was annexed. In 1528 Islam came at last to Ibrim when a garrison of Bosnian mercenaries was sent there and was apparently never relieved. The smaller churches were abandoned, filled with rubbish and later overbuilt with houses. Part of the great cathedral was used as a mosque. In the seventeenth century Ibrim experienced a renewal of prosperity. The descendants of the Bosnian soldiers, who had eventually married local Nubian women, were driven out of Ibrim in 1811 by Mamluks fleeing from Muhammad Ali, the ruler of Egypt. A few months later the Mamluks in turn were expelled by Egyptian forces, and Ibrim was finally abandoned.

Among the wealth of finds from Ibrim are not only artifacts and various material items, but also a large number of written documents of all kinds in a variety of languages—Greek, Coptic, Meroitic, Old Nubian, Arabic, and Turkish. One letter from the site mentions the sixth-century king of Nobatia, Silko, who is also known from a graffito in the Temple of Kalabsha.

The most prominent building at Ibrim today is the ruin of the cathedral, which stands on the highest part of the island. Although it was approximately the same size as the other Christian cathedrals in Nubia, which were located further south at Faras and Old Dongola, the cathedral at Ibrim surpassed them in its artistic style of architecture and the quality of its carving. Depending on which end of Ibrim the cruise ship moors, or as the ship approaches or draws away from the island, it is possible to identify some of the architectural features of the cathedral, and the podium on the southeast side of the island is clearly visible. The precise date of the cathedral is unknown, but it was founded some time during the seventh or eighth century. It was built of sandstone blocks with a rubble and mud fill between the inner and outer walls.

The south wall is still standing to a height of five meters, which was probably the original height. Along the north and south walls were six windows with carved wooden sills and lintels. The interior of the church consisted of a wide nave with two narrow aisles on each side. The aisles immediately to the right and left of the nave were separated from it by a row of granite columns, none of which is now standing, while the outer aisles were separated from the inner ones by a row of stone arches, two of which survive on the southern side. At the east end of the nave was a semicircular apse forming the sanctuary, with a small chamber on each side as the sacristy and baptistry. There were also crypts below the church, in one of which was found the reused stela of Amenophis I, as well as the intact burial of the Nubian bishop Timotheos, who was buried with his letters of appointment dated 1372. The roof of the cathedral was probably made of wood and was largely destroyed by fire during the siege in 1173.

In the distance to the east beyond Ibrim, a ruined structure can be seen on the desert edge, which was apparently another small church, with a monk's cell attached, dating to either the seventh or the eighth century.

It is to be hoped that excavation can continue at Ibrim for many years to come, and so reveal more details of the checkered history of this fascinating site.

Abu Simbel

Dramatically rescued in the 1960s from the rapidly rising waters of Lake Nasser, the two rock-cut temples of Ramesses II at Abu Simbel, particularly the Great Temple, have become almost as famous as the tomb of Tutankhamun. In raising the temples sixty-five meters up the cliffs and 210 meters further northwest, every effort was made to create a new setting comparable to the old. This has largely been achieved, and the approach from the lake now·enjoyed by passengers on the cruise ships fully justifies the efforts made in this regard. With the strains of Aida, Scherezade, or Vangelis coming over the public address system as the ship draws in to shore in front of the temples, even the most insensitive observer must be moved. How gratified Ramesses II must be feeling in whatever afterlife he is enjoying!

After different proposals had been put forward for saving Abu Simbel, an Egyptian scheme to cut the temples into blocks of stone and rebuild them on higher ground was the one adopted, in spite of misgivings, especially from archaeologists. An international team of engineers and construction workers from Germany, Italy, France, Sweden and Egypt, under the auspices of UNESCO, with the necessary support personnel, numbering about three thousand people altogether, labored for four and a half years, all year round and through the heat of summer from 1964 to 1968, to complete the salvage of the temples before they were submerged. As the level of the lake rose alarmingly, a coffer dam was built around the temples to keep out the water while they were being dismantled. The Great Temple was sawn up into 807 blocks, the Small Temple into 235, which were stored nearby while the new site was prepared. When the temples were reassembled within a concrete framework, a mortar of cement and sand was used to join the blocks. Great care was taken to reposition the temples with the same alignment as before and almost the same distance apart. Over each of them an artificial hill, a dome of reinforced concrete, was built, its façade covered with sandstone cut from the cliff face where the temples formerly stood, to recreate as closely as possible the original surroundings. The project was completed at a cost of $40 million, paid for by Egypt, the United States, and UNESCO.

It is not known why this particular spot was chosen for such magnificent buildings by those responsible for their construction, the viceroy Iuny and the first king's cup-bearer Asha-hebsed. There does not appear to have been a town, or any kind of settlement in the area, but the two rocky hills in which the temples were cut were sacred to two local deities, the southern one (of the Great Temple) to Horus of Maha, and the northern one (of the Small Temple) to Hathor of Abshek. Construction of the temples started under Iuny, who was viceroy of Nubia during the first decade of Ramesses II's reign, and they were dedicated in Year 24, when the viceroy was Hekanakht. Both these officials left stelae at Abu Simbel with inscriptions recording their contributions to the building of these monuments.

The Great Temple *(plan 8, page 112)*

The Great Temple, which extends forty-eight meters into the mountain, was dedicated to the gods Amun-Re and Re-Harakhti and to the deified Ramesses II. Ptah, the other principal god of Egypt, also appears in the sanctuary. The temple was preceded by a forecourt (A), enclosed on the north and south by mud-brick walls and bounded on the east by the river. The north wall has been partially reconstructed in mud brick to accommodate the stone gateway leading to the Small Temple. The impressive façade of the temple, which is cut to represent a pylon, is fronted by four colossal seated statues of Ramesses II (E–H). In front of these is a terrace (C), inscribed with a dedicatory text, and with alternate statuettes of a falcon and the king along the edge. Those on the south side are incomplete, perhaps because of the collapse of the second colossus. At the northern end of the terrace is a chapel to Re-Harakhti (D), while just beyond the southern end of the terrace is a chapel to Thoth (B: now closed). Various stelae are carved in the rock at the north and south ends of the terrace, and immediately to the right and left of the north and south colossi. There are two free-standing stelae beside the steps leading up to the terrace (1, 2). The most important stela is the one at the south end of the terrace, which is known as the Marriage Stela (3), because it records the marriage in Year 34 of Ramesses II to the daughter of the Hittite king, Hattusil III, as a way of sealing the alliance between Egypt and the Hittites, begun in Year 21 of Ramesses with the signing of the peace treaty between their two nations. The text describes the princess's journey to Egypt during the winter, when Ramesses II prayed to the gods to send good weather for his new bride's journey. The princess brought with her a large entourage and many gifts for her distinguished bridegroom, who was immediately struck by her beauty and made her his Chief Wife, giving her the Egyptian name Maat-Hor-Neferure.

The magnificent seated colossi of the temple façade, each twenty meters high, are true portraits of majesty, showing a benign yet confident expression on the youthful features of the king, who is indeed 'lord of all he surveys.' The king is wearing the short, pleated, formal kilt; on his head the double crown and sacred cobra on top of the striped *nemes* headcloth; the false beard, symbol of authority, attached to his chin; and his hands rest on his knees. Each statue has its own title inscribed on its shoulder, reflecting the divine aspects of Ramesses II's kingship. The titles are, from left to right; 'The Sun of the Rulers,' 'The Ruler of the Two Lands,' 'The

Beloved of Amun,' 'The Beloved of Atum.' Beside the legs of the colossi are smaller statues of members of the royal family. These are, from left to right: by the first colossus, Princess Nebttawi, an unnamed princess, and Princess Bint-Anath; by the second colossus, Queen Mother Mut-Tuy, Prince Amenhirkhopshef, and Queen Nefertari; by the third colossus, Queen Nefertari, Prince Ramesses, and Princess Beketmut; by the fourth colossus, Queen Mother Mut-Tuy, Princess Merytamun, and Queen Nefertari. The bases of the colossi are all inscribed on the front with the names and titles of the king, the *sem iun-mutef* priest standing before them. On the sides of the thrones of the colossi to the right and left of the entrance, Nile gods are depicted tying together the lotus and papyrus plants around the hieroglyphic sign for 'unite' (the *sma-tawi* motif), symbolizing the unification of Upper and Lower Egypt in the person of the king (12, 13). Below are the names of the king and a row of bound prisoners, graphically represented literally under the king's feet, Africans on the south side (10), and Asiatics and a Libyan on the north (11). Libyan prisoners were apparently brought to work on the building of the temple, probably specially press-ganged for this purpose. On the second southern colossus, the headless one on the left side of the entrance passage, are several graffiti inscribed by Greek, Carian, and Phoenician mercenaries, who passed this way in ancient times, as well as the names of more recent travelers. Just under the left knee is an interesting graffito in Ionian Greek left by Greek and Carian mercenaries sent to the Second Cataract by the Twenty-sixth Dynasty pharaoh Psammetichus II under the command of Amasis in 593 BC.

An earthquake in about Year 31 of Ramesses II's reign caused severe damage to the Great Temple. Inside, pillars cracked and one on the north side of the great hall collapsed, as did also the north jamb of the main entrance. The right arm of the colossus to the north of the doorway fell off, but the biggest tragedy was the colossus to the left of the doorway, the upper half of which broke off and fell to the ground. Paser, the then viceroy of Kush, immediately ordered repairs to be made;

the damaged pillars in the great hall were rebuilt and reinforced, the masonry between the last two pillars on the southern side later providing a suitable surface for the Blessing of Ptah inscription in Year 35. The door jamb was restored and the arm of the colossus was put back and supported with blocks of stone. The fallen colossus, however, defeated the restorers, and so the huge fragments were left where they fell. When the temple was moved, the modern engineers decided also to leave the pieces of the colossus where they had lain for over two thousand years. In commemoration of his restoration of the temple, Paser set up a kneeling statue of himself in the temple; this is now in the British Museum. Part of it was found in the great hall and the other part in the second hall.

Above the entrance of the Great Temple is a niche with a large falcon-headed statue of the sun god Re-Harakhti, by his right leg the jackal-headed *user* symbol and by his left the figure of Maat, goddess of truth and justice. This is a rebus for the throne name of Ramesses II, User-Maat-Re, 'Powerful in Justice is Re.' On either side the king is shown in sunk relief offering a figure of Maat to the statue, thus worshiping his own name as well as the sun god. At the top of the façade is a frieze of twenty-two baboons with paws raised to greet the sun god. Below the baboons are two lines of hieroglyphic inscription, the first consisting of the cartouches of Ramesses II flanked by cobras, the second giving the names of the king running in opposite directions from the center: 'Live Horus the Strong Bull Beloved of Truth, King of Upper and Lower Egypt, Powerful in Justice is Re, Chosen of Re, Son of Re Ramesses Beloved of Amun.' The left side ends with the word 'Beloved of Amun-Re, King of the Gods,' the right side with 'Beloved of Re-Harakhti, the Great God,' indicating, as can be seen elsewhere in the temple, that the southern side was dedicated to Amun-Re and the northern side to Re-Harakhti.

The interior of the temple consists of two pillared halls, a vestibule, and a sanctuary. The great hall (eighteen meters long by 16.7 meters wide) has eight pillars, each fronted by an Osiris-statue of the king in the short kilt, his hands crossed on his chest holding the crook and flail scepters; those on the north side are wearing the double crown, those on the south side the Upper Egyptian crown. The sides of the pillars have scenes depicting the king, or occasionally Queen Nefertari or Princess Bint-Anath, offering to various gods. Between the last two pillars on the southern side is the Blessing of Ptah, which records in rather exaggerated language the buildings and gifts dedicated by the king to Ptah of Memphis. The ceiling of the central aisle is painted with flying vultures, although the cartouches between them that contain the king's names are now faded. The ceilings of the side aisles are painted with stars.

The wall reliefs throughout the temple are generally well preserved, the dominant colors being red, yellow and black, colors that were readily available locally, the red and yellow from ocher and black from soot or charcoal. The great hall (I) is decorated with scenes representing the king as the military leader of his people. Traditional smiting scenes occur on the walls to the right and left beside the main entrance, before Amun-Re on the south (15) and Re-Harakhti on the north (18), with a line of royal offspring under each, princes on the right and princesses on the left. Under the princesses on the north side is a graffito, in four columns of hieroglyphs, of Piay, the sculptor, claiming this as his work, a rare artist's signature. (To the left of this is another graffito in two columns of hieroglyphs of the offering-bearer Panufer.) Campaigns against Syrians, Libyans, and Nubians appear on the south wall (16); at the east end, Ramesses is attacking a Syrian fortress from his chariot. The king appears to have two arms and two bows. This has been variously explained as an alteration in the carving, originally plastered and recarved, the subsequent loss of the plaster exposing the earlier version; or a deliberate attempt by the sculptor to give more animation to the pharaoh's actions. The former explanation is the more likely. The king is accompanied by three of his sons, and a herdsman can be seen fleeing with his livestock at the bottom left below the fortress. In the middle of the wall is a dramatic depiction of the king crushing two Libyans; he is trampling on one, while striking the other with his battle-ax. To the right of this scene the king is shown in his chariot driving a group of Nubian prisoners toward the deities on the adjacent wall, while his pet lion runs alongside.

The whole of the north wall of the great hall is taken up by the Battle of Kadesh (19). This historic event in Ramesses II's reign, which was later recorded in most of his major temples, such as Abydos, Luxor, and his mortuary temple at Thebes (the Ramesseum), as well as Abu Simbel, took place in his fifth year as pharaoh (c. 1275 BC). For over ten years, the Hittites of northern Syria had been threatening the northern limits of the Egyptian empire, and finally Ramesses II resolved to take action. The enemy forces of the Hittites and their allies were occupying the town of Kadesh on the River Orontes in Syria, when the Egyptian army marched to meet them and camped nearby. Two enemy spies were captured and beaten for information, although this later proved to be false, as they told the Egyptians that the Hittite army was some distance away. Battle commenced next day before the Egyptians were prepared, part of the force being still on the far side of the river. Ramesses' army was almost routed at the start, and however much he may be criticized today for his subsequent boasting and exaggeration, it should be remembered that this was simply power politics and propaganda, and it must be acknowledged that the king's personal courage seems to have saved the day, or at least saved Egyptian face. Finding themselves greatly outnumbered, the troops in the first advance turned to flee, but Ramesses stood his ground with his bodyguard until the main army regrouped and reinforcements arrived from the west. In the end the battle was indecisive, both sides claiming victory, but the final outcome, sixteen years later, was the first recorded peace treaty in world history. The Egyptian text of the treaty is inscribed in hieroglyphs in the Temple of Amun-Re at Karnak and in the Ramesseum. The Hittite version, written in Babylonian cuneiform on a clay tablet, was found at the site of the Hittite capital of Hattusas, modern Bogazkoy in Turkey.

The pictorial record of the Battle of Kadesh in the Great Temple of Abu Simbel is like a gigantic comic strip. Reading from left to right, the first episode shows the arrival of the Egyptian army at their camp. A lively picture is given of the camp, which is surrounded by a stockade of shields. To the right is the royal tent decorated with the king's cartouches, and all around is much activity: horses are being fed, soldiers are resting or preparing their weapons, a doctor attends to a wounded officer, servants are busy, and the king's pet lion is being tended by a keeper. In the next scene the seated king is holding a council of war with his officers and officials; his Sherden bodyguard appear below, while the enemy spies are being beaten. The battle itself follows, with all the confusion and melee, and Ramesses in the thick of it; chariots and horses charging; dead and wounded falling in all directions, some drowning in the river along with their horses; the fortress of Kadesh surrounded by the river at the top left of the picture. To the right the king in his chariot is receiving the severed hands of the enemy slain (the usual way of making a tally of the enemy dead), and receiving prisoners.

On either side of the doorway to the second hall are scenes of the king presenting prisoners to the gods, again with the correct orientation: Nubian captives to Amun-Re, the deified Ramesses, and the goddess Mut on the south side (17); Hittite prisoners to Re-Harakhti, the deified Ramesses, and the lioness-headed goddess Iusas, on the north (20). In the southern scene the alteration and recarving of the figures is noticeable, as elsewhere in the temple, where Mut was originally shown seated behind Amun-Re, but with the later insertion of the king, the goddess has been forced to stand! It is interesting to note that when Ramesses II is depicted as a deified king, as he is here, he usually has the ram's horn of Amun curled around his ear (this can also be seen in depictions of Alexander the Great, after he had visited the oracle of Amun in Siwa Oasis). Doorways in the side walls of the great hall give access to long, narrow side-chambers (M) used for storage, perhaps of Nubian tribute, as well as the items belonging to the temple.

These chambers are all carved with offering scenes, and some have a shelf cut out of the rock.

The second hall (J) contains four pillars decorated with carved scenes of the king with different gods. The side walls depict Ramesses II and Queen Nefertari offering to the sacred bark of Amun-Re carried by officials on the south wall (23), and on the north wall the sacred bark of Ramesses himself carried by priests (26). The east and west walls have scenes of the king with other deities, more alterations being visible.

At the rear of the hall three doorways lead to the vestibule (K), the central one opposite the sanctuary (L), which is flanked by two small, undecorated chambers. At the back of the sanctuary are four statues cut in the rock: from left to right, Ptah, Amun-Re, Ramesses II, and Re-Harakhti. They are reasonably well preserved apart from the faces, which have been erased, and Ptah has lost his head. In front of the statues is a pedestal, probably for the sacred bark of the deified king. Relief carvings of the kind usually found in a sanctuary occur on the side walls.

Twice a year, on February 21 and October 21, the rays of the rising sun shine directly into the sanctuary and illuminate the statues. It is not known if the temple was deliberately positioned for this to happen on those particular dates, as there are no ancient records whatsoever that provide evidence for any connection with Ramesses II's accession or his birthday (the occasions commonly cited today in association with this phenomenon), or any other significant date of his reign. A modern Festival of the Sun is sometimes held at Abu Simbel to 'celebrate' these events.

The Dome

Passing through the stone gateway in the northern mud-brick wall beside the Great Temple, a small door to the left in the side of the artificial mountain gives access to the inside of the vast dome of reinforced concrete that covers and protects the temple. However much one admires the skill of the ancient Egyptians in hewing the temple from the mountainside in the first place, one must also acknowledge the expertise of the modern engineers in cutting up, moving, and reconstructing this temple and its companion so skillfully and in creating this huge structure, twenty-five meters high and sixty-five meters across. Part way along the raised walkway through the dome are some plans and diagrams giving statistics about how the temples were moved. The walkway leads to an access tunnel at the back of the dome, which emerges near the ticket kiosk and the car park. A similar dome covers the Small Temple but is not accessible to visitors.

The Small Temple *(plan 9, page 117)*

Approximately one hundred meters north of the Great Temple is the smaller temple dedicated to Hathor of Abshek, a local form of the goddess of love, beauty, and motherhood, and to Queen Nefertari, favorite chief wife of Ramesses II. This was not the first time that a temple in Nubia had been dedicated to a queen, as Amenophis III had built the Temple of Sedeinga, south of the Second Cataract, for his wife Queen Tiye about 150 years earlier. Like the Great Temple, the Small Temple is cut entirely from the rock; it penetrates twenty-four meters into the mountain.

The imposing façade consists of six colossal statues of the king and queen (A–F), each ten meters high, which stand in recesses formed by sloping buttresses. Although this is the queen's temple, only two of the six statues are hers, but they are the same height as those of the king to show that she is of equal status. The queen wears the traditional Hathor headdress of cow-horns, surmounted by a sun-disk with two plumes, and holds against her breast the sistrum-rattle, symbol of Hathor. The king wears various crowns, including on the northernmost colossus the horned and plumed *atef* crown. The horizontal line of inscription above the colossi gives the titles of the king's statues, as with the colossi of the Great Temple: 'The Sun of the Rulers' and 'The Beloved of Atum' on the right; 'The Ruler of the Two Lands' and 'The Beloved of Amun' on the left. Small statues of some of the royal children stand on either side of their parents, princes beside Ramesses and princesses beside Nefertari. From left to right on the southern side of the entrance they are: the princes Meryatum and Meryre, the princesses Merytamun and Henttawi, and the princes Amenhirkhopshef and Rahirwenemef. To the north of the entrance are the same children in reverse. On the buttresses is a dedicatory inscription stating that Ramesses II has cut the temple from the mountain in Nubia for his chief wife, Nefertari, for whom the sun shines, the like of which had never been done before. The projecting piece of rock above the entrance may originally have been intended to be carved into a figure of Hathor, but this was not carried out.

The interior of the temple consists of a pillared hall, vestibule, and sanctuary. The hall (G) has six pillars, which are carved on the central aisle with the Hathor-headed handle and sounding box of the sistrum, and figures of the king and gods on the other three sides. The face of Hathor aptly reflects her role as the goddess of beauty. The colors of the wall reliefs are also well preserved in this temple and red, yellow, and black again predominate. Ramesses inevitably appears frequently in his queen's temple, but the only warlike scenes are on the east wall, with the customary smiting of captives (2, 8). In these and other scenes he is accompanied by Nefertari, who is also shown alone in several scenes offering to a goddess. The style of art in the Small Temple has a different quality to that of the Great Temple; it has altogether a more gentle, feminine aspect, in contrast to the vigor and power of the other. Flowers are frequently shown being offered to the various deities.

On the south wall is a scene of Ramesses II being crowned by Horus of Maha and Seth of Nubet (Ombos, north of Aswan, his Upper Egyptian cult center as a god of power). It is interesting to see Seth here in his role as a god who protects the pharaoh, as opposed to the god of evil. The family of Ramesses II came from the eastern Delta, where Seth was the patron deity, and the king's father was named Seti, 'the one of Seth.'

One of the most charming scenes to be found in any temple is on the east wall of the vestibule (H) to the right of the central doorway (15). The graceful figure of Nefertari is standing between the goddesses Hathor of Abshek and Isis Mother of the Gods, by whom she is being crowned. The slender figures of the women, and the delicate gestures of the goddesses, make this a true work of art with timeless appeal. The corresponding scene to the left of the doorway (19) shows the king, accompanied by Nefertari, presenting flowers to Taweret, here shown as a woman with Hathor-style headdress, instead of her more usual form of a pregnant hippopotamus. Taweret was goddess of pregnancy and childbirth.

At the north and south ends of this transverse vestibule is a small, undecorated chamber, over the doorway of which is a relief carving of the divine Hathor cow in a papyrus thicket being worshiped by the queen on the south (17) and the king on the north (20). In the center is the sanctuary (I). On the back wall the Hathor cow is carved as if emerging from the mountain, a figure of Ramesses II under her chin and a sistrum on either side of her. To her left the king is shown offering her flowers. The cow figure is not exactly in the middle of the back wall but to the right of center, and there are in fact a number of slight changes in alignment throughout the temple, for example between the façade and the pillared hall and between the hall and the vestibule, perhaps caused by the condition of the rock when the temple was being hewn out. The wall scenes in the sanctuary depict the king or queen with different gods, that on the north wall being noteworthy, as it shows Ramesses II burning incense and pouring a libation before his deified self and Queen Nefertari, who is therefore deified along with him.

The Stelae

Set into the rock face to the north and south of the two Abu Simbel temples are several stelae that were salvaged from their original locations and reinstalled here in approximately the same positions. Immediately to the north of the Small Temple is the stela of the viceroy of Kush, Iuny, who was responsible for starting the construction of the temples. Iuny holds out his feather-fan toward the enthroned Ramesses II. To the right is the stela of the first royal cup-bearer, Asha-hebsed, who was in charge of the workmen. The official addresses the king, while the inscriptions tell of Ramesses's decision to build the new temple and to put Asha-hebsed in charge.

To the south of the Great Temple is the stela of Hekanakht, who was viceroy of Kush when the temples were dedicated in Year 24 of Ramesses II's reign. The upper part of the stela shows the king with Princess Merytamun offering to Amun-Re, Re-Harakhti, and the deified Ramesses II, while the lower part shows Hekanakht kneeling before Queen Nefertari. Further to the south is a double stela showing Ramesses II smiting enemies before Amun-Re and Horus of Buhen, with Setau, the viceroy of Kush who built the temples of Gerf Hussein and Wadi al-Sebua for the king, depicted below.

Nubian Temples Abroad

During the Nubian Rescue Campaign, it was decided that some of the smaller monuments would be given to countries that had participated in the campaign, in gratitude for their outstanding contributions, both practical and financial. Eventually five monuments were donated and have become cultural ambassadors abroad for the splendors of ancient Nubia.

Dabod

The Temple of Dabod is now in Madrid, Spain. The temple was built in the Ptolemaic Period by the Meroitic king Azekheramun at Dabod, about sixteen kilometers south of Aswan, and extensions were added in the later Ptolemaic and Roman periods. The temple, which was originally dedicated to Amun, the god of Thebes and Meroe, consists of a forecourt, chapel, and sanctuary, with two gates that were built in front of the temple to form a processional way. The first gate was built during the reign of Ptolemy VI and Cleopatra II, between 172 and 170 BC, when more prominence was given to the goddess Isis, as can also be seen in the forecourt, which was decorated in the early Roman Period. The Temple of Dabod had a quay on the Nile at its original location, and may have been a way-station for the journey of Isis of Philae through her estate in Lower Nubia. The Temple of Dendur and the Kiosk of Qertassi may have been similar stations.

The only suitable place found for the temple when it reached its new European home in 1965 was in a public park. Picturesque as this location may be, the temple is now showing considerable signs of wear after exposure to more extremes of weather than it experienced in Egypt, and concern has been expressed over its condition.

Taffa

Now in the Rijksmuseum van Oudheden in Leiden, the Netherlands, this little temple stood in the town of Taffa, about fifty kilometers south of Aswan and not far north of Kalabsha. The temple consists of a single chamber with six finely carved floral columns, and is undecorated. On the north side of the interior is a recess for a shrine or offering-table. The entrance of the temple is on the south side and is decorated with an elaborate cornice. The building is in almost perfect condition, but there are no inscriptions that would help to date it. Certain factors, however, indicate that it was built in the Greco-Roman Period. There was originally a quay on the Nile in front of the temple.

Dendur

The Temple of Dendur was situated on the west bank of the Nile close to the river, about twenty kilometers south of Kalabsha, and was apparently in the middle of a town, as it was surrounded by ruins of domestic buildings. Nowadays housed in the purpose-built Sackler Wing in the Metropolitan Museum of Art, New York, the temple dates to the Roman Period and the reign of Augustus, and was dedicated to two brothers, Petisis and Pehorus, sons of a local Nubian chieftain, as well as the goddess Isis.

The temple consists of a pronaos, vestibule, and sanctuary, fronted by a stone gate that originally stood in a mud-brick enclosure wall. The temple was built against a rocky hillside, where a small chamber had been cut in the rock, which may have been the burial place of one or both of the brothers. The walls inside and out are decorated with carved reliefs showing the Roman emperor offering to the two brothers, as well as Isis and other deities. With Dabod and Qertassi, Dendur may have been on the processional route for the divine image of Isis of Philae. The temple became a Christian church in the sixth century AD.

Al-Lesiya

The small rock-cut temple of al-Lesiya was given to Italy after the Nubian Campaign and is now in the Turin Museum. It was originally cut out of the cliffs on the east bank of the Nile about four kilometers north of Qasr Ibrim and one kilometer back from the river bank. The temple dates to the reign of Tuthmosis III (c. 1450 BC), and consists of a hall with a niche at the rear. Horus of Miam (ancient Aniba, which was on the west bank opposite) is the god most frequently portrayed, which leads to the conclusion that the temple was dedicated to him. Other deities are also represented, both Nubian and Egyptian, including the deified Senusert III, Horus of Buhen, and Hathor of Abshek. Kneeling figures of Setau, viceroy of Kush in the time of Ramesses II, were added to scenes in the niche, which contains three much damaged statues, perhaps of Tuthmosis III with Horus of Miam and another god.

Ptolemaic Gateway from Kalabsha

During the dismantling of the Temple of Kalabsha by German archaeologists in 1962–63, a large number of stones were found as filling in the walls of the sanctuary and some also in the foundations, a total of about 250 blocks. Miraculously, many of these stones were well preserved, some with color surviving.

About a hundred of them came from a small shrine built by Ptolemy IX, with further decoration carried out under Augustus Caesar. This was reconstructed on the southern tip of the island of Elephantine at Aswan by the German Archaeological Institute in Cairo.

About a hundred more stones were from a large gateway also built in the Ptolemaic Period and decorated under Augustus, who appears in the reliefs. Approximately 80 percent of the blocks from the gateway were recovered, and in 1971 these were given to the Federal Republic of Germany in recognition of their contribution to the Nubian Rescue Campaign. The gateway was reconstructed in the Egyptian Museum, Berlin. The sandstone gateway, which is over seven meters high, originally stood in a mud-brick wall, and had a large one-leaf wooden door. It is decorated with carved reliefs on the outer and inner sides of the doorway as well as in the passage. The titles of Augustus, which are in an early form, and other aspects of the hieroglyphic inscriptions, indicate that the gateway was built late in the Ptolemaic Period and the decoration was completed during the reign of the first Roman pharaoh of Egypt. The scenes show Augustus before various deities, including Isis, Osiris, and Mandulis, the local god of Kalabsha.

The Nubia Museum, Aswan

In November 1997, the long-awaited Nubia Museum was opened. It is a celebration of Nubian history and culture from its earliest beginnings until the building of the High Dam. The museum is located on the road to the airport, opposite the Fatimid cemetery, its sandstone building, which incorporates features of traditional Nubian architecture, blending well into its rocky surroundings. The entrance is on the road leading past the Cataract Hotel to the Basma Hotel.

The museum is on two levels, with a lecture room, a temporary exhibition hall for special displays, and a gift shop on the ground floor, and the main exhibition hall on the lower level. The museum also has classrooms and an open-air theater, as well as an attractive garden, where various items are on display, including a reconstruction of a cave with prehistoric rock carvings, and a full-size Nubian village house with its characteristic decoration.

The main exhibition hall has as its impressive centerpiece a colossal statue of Ramesses II from his temple at Gerf Hussein, which was in too poor a condition to be saved in its entirety. Moving in a clockwise direction, the visitor can see explanatory panels and displays illustrating the birth of the Nile, Nubia in the prehistoric and new Stone Ages, the Old and Middle Kingdoms, the Kingdom of Kush, Egyptian civilization in Nubia, the Twenty-fifth Dynasty, Meroe, Christian and Islamic Nubia, Irrigation, the UNESCO Campaign, and a diorama of Nubian village life and folklore. Many of the objects on display were salvaged from Nubia since the beginning of this century and have been brought from storerooms, as well as from the Elephantine Museum at Aswan and the Egyptian, Coptic, and Islamic Museums in Cairo.

Among the most important items in the collection are stone tools, cosmetic palettes, pottery, and ivory pieces from the prehistoric period and A-group and C-group cultures; statues, offering-tables, and other items from the Elephantine shrine of Heka-ib and other Governors of Aswan; the reconstructed rock-cut shrine of Usersatet, viceroy of Kush under Amenophis II, from Qasr Ibrim; a mummified ram of Khnum with a gold mask from the Temple of Khnum on Elephantine; statuettes of eminent Nubians found at Karnak; the Piye stela; the head of a statue of Taharka; a pair statue of a Meroitic queen and prince; relief carvings from the temple of Ramesses II at Gerf Hussein and the chapel of Horemheb at Abu Oda; a Meroitic lion and other items from Qasr Ibrim; treasures from the tombs and horse burials at Ballana and Qustul; and Christian frescoes from the Church of Abdallah Nerqe. The museum already has almost two thousand items on display and is designed to house a further thousand.

Plans

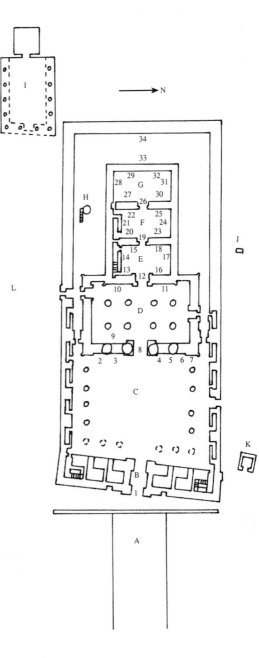

1: The Temple of Kalabsha

A. Causeway.
B. Pylon.
C. Open court.
D. Pronaos — hypostyle hall.
E. Outer vestibule.
F. Inner vestibule.
G. Sanctuary.

H. Nilometer.
I. Chapel of Dedwen.
J. Stela of Psammetichus II.
K. Ptolemaic Chapel.
L. Petroglyphs, blocks from
   Gerf Hussein, and stela of
   Seti I from Ibrim.

1. Pylon entrance. Above, winged sun-disk; lintel, double-scene, part destroyed, l: king offers to Mandulis, Osiris, Isis; r: king before Harsiesi, Mandulis, Wadjet; r jamb, Horus graffito, Coptic crosses, graffiti; passage, r: Augustus before Horus; inner lintel and jambs, king offers to Mandulis, Osiris, Isis, Horus.
2. King before child Mandulis, Isis.
3. King purified by Horus and Thoth; Harsiesi behind.
4. Greek inscription of Besarion; Mandulis, Isis, falcon graffito below.
5. Column: Meroitic inscription of King Kharamadeye.
6. Unfinished carving of two gods.
7. Graffito of Silko, king of Nobatia.
8. Doorway to hypostyle hall; above, winged sun-disk; lintels and jambs, Isis, Mandulis, Harsiesi, Osiris, Wadjet.
9. Christian crosses.
10. L–r: 1st row: king offers crowns to Horus of Edfu, Mandulis; Maat to Hathor, Harpocrates, sphinx beyond; 2nd row: Ptolemy offers field to Isis, Mandulis, Horus; Khnum before Re-Harakhti; Amenophis II offers wine to Min-Re, Mandulis; 3rd row: king offers sacred eye to Osiris, Isis with Horus, Mandulis; field to Mandulis, Isis; 4th row: Horus before Harpocrates, Mandulis, and another god; king before Isis, Mandulis; Isis before Mandulis as bird beyond. Base: king followed by nine Nile-gods.
11. R–l: 1st row: king smites enemy before Horus, Shu, Tefnut; offers incense to Mandulis, Wadjet; 2nd row: king with field-goddess before Osiris, Mandulis; Isis, Mandulis, Horus; 3rd row: king presents offerings to Amun, Thoth, Khonsu, offers cloth to child Mandulis, Hathor; 4th row: damaged (only crowns remaining), king before Isis, child Mandulis, Horus, and one other god; offers to Mandulis as bird in lotus-clump, Isis. Base: king followed by eight Nile-gods before Mandulis.
12. Doorway to outer vestibule: above, winged sun-disk; lintel, double-scene, l: Trajan offers to Mandulis, Osiris, Isis; r: king offers to Horus, Mandulis, Wadjet; jambs, Mandulis and gods; inner end,

lintel damaged, double-scene, l: king runs with vases and flail to
Mandulis, Wadjet; r: runs to Osiris, Isis, Horus; jambs, l: king
offers to Isis, Pharaoh of Senmet (Bigeh), Osiris, Isis; r: offers to
Mandulis, Shu.

13. 1st row: king offers wine to Re-Harakhti, Hathor; 2nd row
    (unfinished): king offers to Shu, Tefnut; 3rd row: part of
    inscription.

14. 1st row: king offers incense to Osiris, Isis, Horus; field to Isis and
    child Mandulis; 2nd row: king offers incense to Geb, Nut,
    Mandulis; sacred eye to Horus, Mandulis, Wadjet; 3rd row: king
    purified by Thoth, Horus; crowned by Wadjet, Nekhbet; led by
    Mandulis, Montu (continued on adjacent wall, no.15).

15. 1st and 2nd rows: king presents prisoners to Isis; offers wine to
    Osiris, Mandulis; 3rd row: (continued from no.14) Osiris, Isis,
    Mandulis.

13–15. Base: king followed by nome-gods before Osiris, Isis, Horus.

16. 1st row: king offers field to Isis, Mut; brazier to Khnum; 2nd
    row: king offers vase to Khnum, Hathor; sacred eye to Mandulis;
    3rd row: king offers incense, libation to Mandulis, Wadjet; milk to
    Mandulis.

17. 1st row: king uplifts sky before Ptah in shrine, Sekhmet,
    Mandulis; offers Maat to Thoth, Nehemawat, Mandulis; 2nd row:
    king offers lettuces to Min, Isis, Mandulis; incense, libation to
    Mandulis, Wadjet; 3rd row: king in procession with standards and
    priest; purified by Thoth, Horus; crowned by Wadjet, Nekhbet
    (compare same on opposite wall).

18. 1st row: king offers wine to Mandulis, worships Mandulis,
    Wadjet; 2nd row: king offers incense to Mandulis; milk to
    Mandulis, Wadjet; 3rd row: king led by Mandulis and falcon-headed
    god to two forms of Mandulis, Wadjet.

16–18. Base: king followed by nome-gods before Mandulis, child
    Mandulis, Wadjet. Frieze: inscription with cartouches of Augustus.

19. Doorway to Inner Vestibule: above, winged sun-disk; lintel and
    jambs on inner and outer ends, king offers to Horus, Osiris, Isis,
    Mandulis, Wadjet, Nephthys. Base (outer): two Nile-gods on each
    side.

20. 1st row: king presents prisoners to Isis, Satis; 2nd row: king offers
    incense, libation to Osiris, Mandulis.

21. 1st row: king offers incense, libation to Osiris, Isis, Horus,
    Mandulis, Wadjet; 2nd row: king offers incense to lion-headed
    Tutu; offerings to Osiris, Isis, child Mandulis; incense to Imhotep.

22. 1st row: king offers libation to Osiris, Isis; 2nd row: king offers
    food to Isis, Mandulis.

0–22. Base: king followed by Nile-gods and field-goddesses offers to Osiris, Isis, Horus.

3. 1st row: king (damaged) before Mandulis, Thoth; offers incense to Mandulis, ram-headed Amun; 2nd row: king offers wine to Arsenuphis, Tefnut; milk to Mandulis, Arsenuphis.

4. 1st row: king offers vase to Khnum, Satis, child Mandulis on lotus; Maat to Amun of Napata, Amun of Primis; 2nd row: king offers wine, then offerings, to Mandulis, child Mandulis.

5. 1st row: king offers libation to child Mandulis, Mandulis, Wadjet; 2nd row: king offers incense, libation to Mandulis; bread to Mandulis, Wadjet.

3–25. Base: king followed by Nile-gods and field-goddesses offers to Mandulis, child Mandulis, Wadjet.

6. Doorway to sanctuary: cornice and lintel, winged sun-disks.

7. 1st row: king offers to Osiris, Isis, Mandulis, Wadjet; 2nd row: king before Isis, Mandulis; offers sacred eye to child Mandulis.

8. 1st row: king offers crowns to Horus, Hathor, child Mandulis; Maat to Montu, Re-Harakhti, Thenent, Mandulis; 2nd row: king offers to Osiris, Isis, Mandulis; worships child Mandulis, Nekhbet, Wadjet.

9. L–r: 1st row: king offers lotuses to Isis, Harpocrates; milk and then cloth to child Mandulis, Wadjet.

7–29. Base: king followed by Nile-gods offers vases to Osiris, Mandulis.

0. 1st row: king offers mirrors to Isis, Hathor, wreath to Mandulis, Wadjet; 2nd row: king offers wine to Mandulis, child Mandulis; vases to child Mandulis, Wadjet.

1. 1st row: king offers vases to Khnum, Satis, child Mandulis; Maat to Amun-Re, Mut, Horus; 2nd row: king with queen offers Maat to Osiris, Isis, Nephthys, wine to Horus, Hathor, Mandulis.

2. R–l: 1st row: king offers lotuses to Mandulis, Wadjet; cloth to child Mandulis, goddess; milk to Mandulis, Wadjet; 2nd row: king offers lotuses to Isis, Harpocrates; ointment to Mandulis, Wadjet; incense to Isis, Horus.

0–32. Base: king followed by Nile-gods offers vases to Isis, Mandulis.

3. Double-scene (incomplete): l: king offers incense to Isis, Horus, Mandulis; r: king censes before Osiris, Isis, Horus; base: king offers field to Mandulis, two gods; graffiti of Mandulis-birds, goddesses.

4. King (on right) before Mandulis with offering-stand between them.

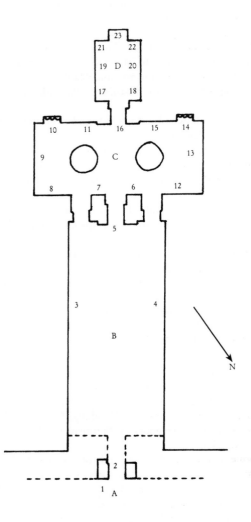

2: The Temple of Beit al-Wali

A. Stone gate in mud-brick
  pylon.
B. Forecourt.

C. Vestibule.
D. Sanctuary.

1. Doorway, jambs: Ramesses II.
2. Passage, l, r: cartouches of Ramesses II.
3. Two scenes: l: king and two sons in chariots charge Nubians, left
   end: Nubian camp under doum-palms; r: king in pavilion receives
   Nubian tribute.
4. Five scenes, r–l: king with Asiatic captives receives prisoners from
   prince; attacks Syrian fortress; charges Asiatics in chariot; king with
   dog smites Libyan; king in pavilion receives prince and officials with
   prisoners.
5. Doorway to vestibule: above, double-scene damaged, king before a
   god; lintel, double-scene, king runs with oar and *hap* to Amun-Re;
   jambs, l: king before Horus; r: king before Mut, Khonsu. Passage, l:
   king receives life from Amun-Re; r: from Mut; inner end, l: Messuy,
   viceroy of Kush under Merenptah.
6. King embraced by Horus of Miam.
7. King receives life from Atum.
8. King smites Nubian.
9. King with Hathor offers incense and libation to Horus of Buhen
   and Isis as scorpion-goddess.
10. Niche: statues of king between Horus of Baki, Isis; l: royal titles.
11. King offers Maat to Amun-Re.
12. King smites Libyan.
13. King with Anukis offers wine to Khnum, Satis.
14. Niche: statues of king between Khnum and Anukis; royal titles at
    right.
15. King offers wine to Amun-Re.
16. Doorway to sanctuary: lintel, double-scene, king before Amun-Re;
    jambs, l: king offers Maat to Amun-Re and bread to Sokar; r: king
    offers wine to Amun-Re, Horus of Baki; passage, l: king embraced
    by Satis; r: embraced by goddess Miket (much damaged).
17. Isis suckles young Ramesses II.
18. Anukis suckles young Ramesses II.
19. King offers wine to Horus of Baki, incense, libation to Amun-Re.
20. King led by Satis and Khnum, offers incense to Amun-Re.
21. Min-Amun.
22. Ptah in shrine.
23. Niche: three original statues completely destroyed.

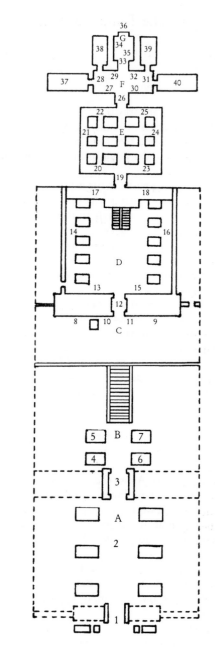

3: The Temple of Wadi al-Sebua

A. First court.
B. Second court.
C. Pylon.
D. Open court.

E. Pillared hall.
F. Vestibule.
G. Sanctuary.

1. Outer Gate: royal names and titles; passage, r: king, Horus.
2. Six sphinxes in double crown; bases: front, *iunmutef* priest before king's cartouches; sides and back, l (south side): Nubian prisoners; r (north side): Asiatic, Libyan prisoners.
3. Inner Gate: royal names, titles; jambs, king, gods.
4–7. Falcon-headed sphinxes in double crown with statuette of king in front.
4. Horus of Maha.
5. Horus of Miam.
6. Horus of Baki.
7. Horus of Edfu.
8. King smiting prisoners before Amun-Re.
9. King smiting prisoners before Re-Harakhti.
10–11. Nome-goddesses offering to king's cartouches.
12. Pylon doorway: lintel, double-scene, king with goddess and Montu; king offers wine to Amun-Re each side; jambs, l: king offers to Amun-Re (god destroyed); r: king offers to Amun-Re, Re-Harakhti, Atum. Passage: king and names, Re-Harakhti on left. Inner lintel, double-scene, king before Amun-Re, deified Ramesses II; jambs, l: mostly destroyed; r: king offers to Ptah, Onuris, Re-Harakhti.
13. King before Amun-Re, Mut; before Re-Harakhti, Hathor, Ptah; below, 20 princesses.
14. Eight scenes: king offers to deified Ramesses II (twice), Horus, Amun and Mut, Ptah, lioness-goddess, and is taken by Horus to Amun-Re, Mut; below, 25 princes, 9 princesses.
15. King offers to Re-Harakhti, Iusas; is taken by two gods to Khnum; below, 18 princesses.
16. Eight scenes: first three mostly destroyed, then: king offers to falcon-headed god; to Re-Harakhti; to Amun, Mut; king on unity sign with two Horus figures; king, Hathor before Atum, goddess; below, 28 princes, 7 princesses.
17. King with Thoth, Re-Harakhti; king offers Maat to Amun-Re, Ramesses II.
18. King and deified Ramesses II before Amun, Mut; king offers to Re-Harakhti, Ramesses II.

Osirid pillars: (much eroded), royal titles; rear side, two scenes, king with deity.

19. Doorway to pillared hall: lintel and jambs, king offers to Horus, Amun, Mut, Re-Harakhti, Wadjet; captives below. Passage: royal names and titles; l: king offers Maat to Amun-Re.
20. King offers to Ptah, deified Ramesses II, Hathor.
21. Two rows (parts destroyed): king offers to sacred barks.
22. King offers Maat to Amun, deified Ramesses II, Khonsu.
23. King offers to Onuris-Shu, Tefnut, Nekhbet.
24. 1st row (parts destroyed): king before Amun-Re, Ptah, Re-Harakhti, goddess; 2nd row (parts destroyed): king with Atum, Montu; before Amun, Mut, Khonsu; purified by Thoth, Re-Harakhti.
25. (Parts destroyed) deified Ramesses II, Atum.

Pillars (damaged), royal titles, king before deities including Satis, Anubis, Nekhbet, Amaunet, Khnum, Montu, Horus, Re-Harakhti, Min.

26. Doorway to vestibule: lintels and jambs, king offers to gods including Amun, Mut, Re-Harakhti. Passage, l: king offers flowers to a god.
27. King censing before Ptah, deified Ramesses II, cow-headed Hathor.
28. L: king receives life from Horus of Miam; r: receives life from Horus of Buhen.
29. King offers wine to Amun, Khonsu, Mut.
30. King censing before Onuris-Shu, deified Ramesses II, Tefnut, Nekhbet.
31. L: king receives life from Khnum; r: receives life from Horus of Baki.
32. King offers wine to Re-Harakhti, deified Ramesses II, Iusas.
33. Doorway to sanctuary: lintel and jambs, king and gods. Passage, royal names, titles; l: king receives life from Re-Harakhti. Above inner doorway, king offers to sphinx.
34. Right of doorway: king embraced by Mut; south wall, king censing before bark of Amun-Re.
35. Left of doorway: king embraced by Hathor; north wall, king offers flowers to bark of Re-Harakhti.
36. Above niche, king worships bark of Re-Harakhti with apes; l & r: king with flowers. Inside niche, Christian painting of St. Peter on plaster.

37. L wall, six scenes: king offers wine to Amun-Re; incense to Mut; vases to Khonsu; flowers to Re-Harakhti; cobra to Sekhmet; wine to Amun-Re. R wall, five scenes: king offers name to Ptah, deified Ramesses II, Hathor; incense to Horus of Baki; bread to Horus of Miam; bread to Horus of Buhen; wine to Atum.

38. L wall, four scenes: king receives scepters from Horus of Miam; offers incense to Amun-Re, deified Ramesses II, Mut; wine to Amun-Re-Kamutef, Isis; incense to Horus of Buhen. R wall, five scenes: king offers 'jubilee' symbol to Horus of Baki; vases to Re-Harakhti, deified Ramesses II; wine to Amun-Re; ointment to Mut; feather to Khnum.

39. L wall, four scenes: king receives life from Isis; king with *ka* offers lettuces to Amun-Re-Kamutef, Mut, Khonsu; incense and libation to Re-Harakhti; bread to Amun-Re.

40. L wall, five scenes: king offers flowers to Shu; cartouche to Tefnut; wine to Geb; incense to Nut; wine to Osiris. R wall, five scenes: king offers bread to Montu; bread to Raettawi; statue to Atum; incense to Nebethetepet; wine to Ptah.

Doorways to side-chambers (37–40): above, king and deities; lintel, two sphinxes; jambs, royal titles; passage, king and god.

41. Five scenes (much of first destroyed): king with Atum and three other gods; offers to Min-Amun; to Re-Harakhti; to Ptah; offers Maat to Amun, Re-Harakhti.

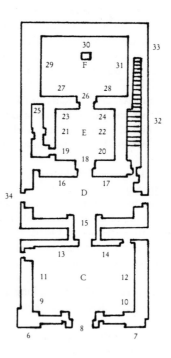

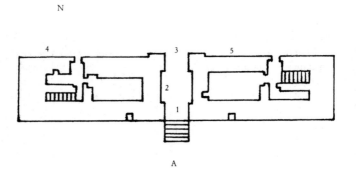

4: The Temple of Dakka

A. Pylon.

B. Open court.

C. Pronaos.

D. Vestibule.

E. Chapel of Arkamani.

F. Roman sanctuary.

1. Pylon entrance: above, winged sun-disk; jambs, Horus sketches.
2. 1st row: king before Thoth, Tefnut, Hathor; 2nd row: king offers field to Isis (Meroitic graffito).
3. Doorway inner end: above, winged sun-disk.
4. Sketch of woman, cow, calf; unfinished carving of god, offering-table.
5. Sketch of Horus; unfinished carving of Osiris, Isis.
6. 1st row destroyed; 2nd row: Ptolemy VII before god, goddess (both headless); 3rd row: Ptolemy VII before Khnum, Hathor; base: Ptolemy VII, Cleopatra III followed by Nile-god, field-goddess.
7. 1st row destroyed; 2nd row: Ptolemy VII before Horus, Hathor; 3rd row: Ptolemy VII offers field to Osiris, Isis; base: Ptolemy VII, Cleopatra III followed by Nile-god, field-goddess.
8. Frieze above facade (part destroyed) with cartouches of Ptolemy VII and winged scarab.
9–10. Four sacred cobras (uraei).
11. 1st row: king offers incense, libation to Amun of Napata, Amun of Primis, Horus, Meroitic king beyond; 2nd row: king offers symbols to Osiris, Isis (and Horus); palette to Thoth of Hermopolis, Thoth of Pnubs, Tefnut; 3rd row: scenes destroyed by later doorway.
12. 1st row destroyed; 2nd row, r: king offering (rest of row destroyed); 3rd row: Augustus presenting offerings.
13. Lower row: Augustus offers field to Isis, Horus; king offers milk to (Osiris).
14. All decoration destroyed.
15. Doorway to vestibule: lintel, double-scene, left side, Ptolemy IV with Arsinoe III offers Maat to Thoth of Pnubs, Tefnut; right side much damaged. Jambs, l: Ptolemy IV offers myrrh to Re-Harakhti, food to Khnum-Re, wine to Hathor; r: king offers ointment to Amun-Re, food to Horus, field to Isis; base, unfinished Nile-god. Passage, l: Augustus offers Maat to (Thoth of Pnubs destroyed), Tefnut. Inner side, above, winged sun-disk; lintel, double-scene, Isis gives life to Horus name with cartouches of Ptolemy IV, Arsinoe III, Ptolemy II, Arsinoe II, Ptolemy III, Berenice II; jambs, l: Ptolemy IV worships Satis, presents offerings to Isis; r: (Ptolemy IV) worships Anukis, presents offerings to Hathor. Base: Nile-gods.

16. 1st row: king offers to Thoth, Shu, Arsenuphis; 2nd row: (king destroyed) before Khnum, Hathor, Pharaoh of Senmet (all three headless), Wepset; 3rd row: king presents offerings to Osiris, Isis, Thoth, Tefnut.

17. Partly destroyed. 1st row: king (headless) offers ointment to Osiris, Isis, Horus; 2nd row: king (headless) offers wine to Amun-Re (headless), Mut, Khonsu, Hathor; 3rd row: much destroyed, king presents offerings to Osiris, Isis, Thoth, Tefnut.

16–17. Base: Nile-gods, field-goddesses.

18. Doorway to Chapel of Arkamani: outer side, above, damaged inscription of Arkamani; lintel, double-scene, l: Tiberius with queen offers Maat to Thoth, Tefnut; r: offers same to Osiris, Isis. Jambs, l: king offers to Osiris, incense to Horus, wine to Hathor, field to Isis; r (much damaged): king offers wine to Thoth, sacred eye to Tefnut, censes before Arsenuphis, offers to Shu.

19. 1st row (most destroyed): king offers sistrum to Hathor; 2nd row: king worships Imhotep (latter destroyed from waist up, compare 20, 2nd row); 3rd row: king crowned by Atum, Montu (upper part only).

20. 1st row destroyed; 2nd row: king worships Imhotep; 3rd row: king purified by Thoth, Horus.

21. L–r (left end destroyed by later doorway): 1st row: king (hands only) offers bread to Osiris, Isis, Horus; Maat to Thoth, Wepset; wine to Re-Harakhti, Hathor; 2nd row: king offers Maat to Shu, Tefnut (partially destroyed); flowers to Arsenuphis, Tefnut, incense with hymn to Isis, Harpocrates; 3rd row: king (arms only) offers sacred eye to Min, Nephthys; offerings to Harpocrates, Nekhbet; incense, libation to Osiris. Base: marsh plants. Frieze: winged cobras and *djed* pillars.

22. R–l: 1st row: king (partly destroyed) offers food to Thoth, Nehemawat; libation to Khnum-Re, Satis, Ptah-Nun; ointment to Osiris, Isis; 2nd row: king offers collar to Amun-Re, Nut, Khonsu; water-jar to ram-headed Amun of Dabod, Satis; wine to Pharaoh of Senmet (Bigeh), Anukis; 3rd row: king (headless) offers temple to Thoth, Arsenuphis, Tefnut; offers to Harpocrates, Wadjet; king (destroyed by later doorway) before Thoth.

23. 1st row: king offers Maat to Thoth, Tefnut; 2nd row: king offers food to Horus, Hathor; 3rd row: king offers wine to Isis (inscription concerning Dodekaschoinos).

24. 1st row: king offers cloth to Osiris, Isis; 2nd row: king offers food to Horus of Buhen, Hathor; 3rd row: king offers ointment to Thoth. Frieze: ibises.

25. Roman side-chapel: inner doorway, 'eternity' figure; left wall, 1st row: king offers incense to Arsenuphis, Tefnut; 2nd row: king offers cloth to Osiris, Isis; right wall, 1st row: king offers sacred eye to Horus, Hathor; 2nd row: king offers wine to Thoth, Tefnut; end-wall: 1st row: two ibises on pedestals decorated with lions; 2nd row: Thoth as ape worships Tefnut as lioness; 3rd row: two falcons protect cartouches of pharaoh; 4th row: two seated lions, perhaps representing Shu, Tefnut.

26. Doorway to sanctuary: lintel, center, winged sun-disk; l: king receives life from Thoth; r: receives life from Hathor; jambs, inscriptions, left of Thoth, right of Isis; below, king presents offerings; l, r of jambs, Nekhbet, Wadjet as cobras on papyrus-stem. Inner side: above, apes worshiping winged scarab, inscription of Horus; lintel, winged sun-disk.

27. L–r: Nekhbet as cobra on papyrus-stem; 1st row: king offers incense to Horuses of Baki and Buhen; 2nd row: king presents offerings to Thoth, Tefnut; base: king followed by Nile-gods before two deities.

28. R–l: 1st row: king offers incense to two forms of Horus; 2nd row: king presents offerings to Isis, Harsiesi (demotic graffito); base: king followed by Nile-gods before Thoth as ape under sacred tree.

29. L–r: 1st row: king offers incense; libation to Osiris, Isis; necklace to Thoth, Tefnut; 2nd row: king offers collar to Isis, Harsiesi; sistra to Hathor, Harpocrates.

30. Double-scenes, l: 1st row: king offers scepter to Horus, with ibis on stand below window; offers water-clock to Isis; 2nd row: king offers field to Isis; milk to Osiris, Isis; r: 1st row: king offers collar to Shu, with Thoth as ibis on stand below window; offers wreath to Thoth-Shu; 2nd row: damaged, king offers incense to Arsenuphis, wine to Shu.

31. R–l: 1st row: king offers incense, libation to Thoth, Sekhmet; Maat to Amun-Re, Mut; 2nd row: king offers ointment to Thoth, Tefnut; sphinx-jar to Arsenuphis, Tefnut.

29–31. Base: Nile-gods. Frieze: falcons; cartouche of Pharaoh.

32. Horus, Thoth, Arsenuphis, Tefnut, Hathor.

33. Thoth, Arsenuphis.

34. Lion's head carving on water-spout.

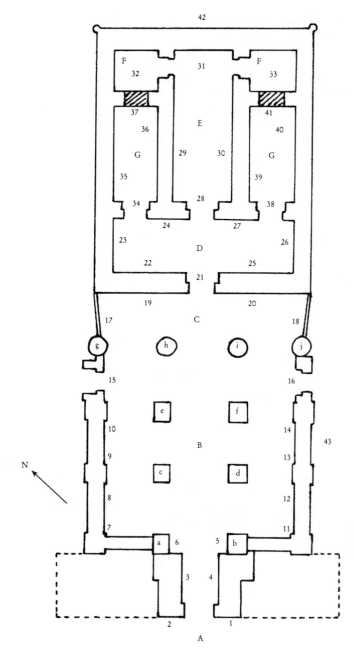

5: The Temple of Amada

Stone gateway in mud-
•rick pylon.
Pillared hall.
Portico.

D. Vestibule.
E. Sanctuary.
F. Cult-chambers.
G. Side-rooms.

Tuthmosis III with Re-Harakhti; below, Viceroy Messuy before
artouches of Merenptah.
Amenophis II with Re-Harakhti; below, Viceroy Messuy before
artouches of Merenptah.
Amenophis before Re-Harakhti, Montu; below, inscription of
Merenptah, Messuy at side.
Viceroy Setau; inscription of Ramesses II.
Titles of Tuthmosis III.
Titles of Amenophis II (erased by Akhenaten, restored by Seti I).
Titles of Tuthmosis IV, 'beloved of Senusert.'
Satis presents Tuthmosis IV to Re-Harakhti.
Thoth presents Tuthmosis to Amun-Re.
Tuthmosis IV embraced by Isis.
Titles of Tuthmosis III.
Tuthmosis IV suckled by Hathor between Khnum and Isis.
Thoth writes king's name on sacred tree; Tuthmosis IV kneels
eneath, before Atum.
Tuthmosis IV embraced by Hathor of Abshek (Abu Simbel).
illars: side facing central aisle, scene of Tuthmosis IV with deity;
ther three sides, inscriptions.
King and Anukis; below, Viceroy Hekanakht (Ramesses II).
King and Khnum; below, Viceroy Hekanakht (Ramesses II).
King and Khepri.
King and Amun.
King and Atum.
King and Ptah.
North doorway (left): jambs, royal titles, serpent each side.
South doorway (right): above, Tuthmosis IV runs with hap and
ar to Amun; lintel, jambs: royal titles. Outer side: on column
apital to right of doorway, Viceroy Messuy (much eroded).
18. Damaged scenes, king before Amun-Re or Re-Harakhti.
Tuthmosis III led by Horus and another god; king embraced by
e-Harakhti, Anukis behind.
Tuthmosis III before Khnum, embraced by Re-Harakhti, before
mun.

Proto-Doric Columns: each column has vertical line of royal titles;
  columns (h), (i), (j) have raised relief carving of goddess.
g. Titles of Amenophis II; (no goddess).
h. Titles of Amenophis II; goddess Nebethetepet.
i. Titles of Tuthmosis III; goddess Iusas.
j. Titles of Tuthmosis III; goddess Sekhmet.

21. Doorway to vestibule. Outer side: jambs, l: Tuthmosis III
  offering; below, Chancellor Bay before cartouches of Siptah;
  inscription of Piay, fan-bearer on right of king; l: Amenophis II
  offering; below, Queen Tausert with sistrum; inscription of Piay.
  Passage: inscription of Seti I. Inner side: inscriptions of Tuthmosis
  III.
22. Amenophis II purified by Thoth, Horus.
23. Amenophis II runs with oar and *hap* to Amun-Re.
24. Re-Harakhti embraces young Amenophis II.
25. Tuthmosis III embraced by Isis; Amenophis II offers incense,
  libation to Amun-Re.
26. Tuthmosis III with Horus of Miam, receives life from Re-
  Harakhti.
27. Amun-Re embraces young Tuthmosis III.
28. Doorway to sanctuary: inscriptions of Tuthmosis III.
29. L–r: Amenophis II with Hathor receives scepters from Re-
  Harakhti, presents offerings to Amun-Re (niche later cut in wall).
30. R–l: Tuthmosis III with Satis receives life from Amun-Re, presen
  offerings to Re (niche later cut in wall).
31. Year 3 inscription of Amenophis II; above, Amenophis in boat
  offers wine to Re-Harakhti, Amun-Re.
32, 33. Side-chambers: Tuthmosis III, Amenophis II with Amun-Re
  Re-Harakhti, Hathor, Horus of Edfu.
34. Doorway to north side-chapel (left): outer side, inscription of
  Amenophis II; inner side, inscription of Tuthmosis III.
35. 1st row: Amenophis II offers milk, incense, libation to Amun-R
  2nd row: king offers bread, wine, offerings to Re-Harakhti.
36. 1st row: Tuthmosis III embraced by Re-Harakhti, before Amun,
  offers vases to Re-Harakhti; scepter to Amun; 2nd row: king with
  Hathor offers flowers, birds to Re; bread, then vases to Re-
  Harakhti.
37. 1st row: Tuthmosis II offers libation to Amun-Re, sistra to
  Hathor; 2nd row destroyed by later doorway.
38. Doorway to south side-chapel (right): outer, inner sides,
  inscription of Tuthmosis III.

39. 1st row: Tuthmosis III offers temple to Amun; marks temple area with Sefkhet-abu; before Amun-Re; embraced by Amun-Re; 2nd row: Tuthmosis runs with flail and scepter to Re-Harakhti; offers temple to Re-Harakhti; incense, libation to Re.

40. 1st row: Amenophis II offers four calves to Amun-Re; presents trussed oxen to Amun-Re, Re; 2nd row: Amenophis II embraced by Horus of Edfu, Re-Harakhti; presents four boxes of colored cloth to Re-Harakhti; runs with vases to Re-Harakhti.

41. 1st row: Amenophis II offers incense to Amun-Re; Tuthmosis III offers wine to Amun-Re; 2nd row destroyed by later doorway.

42. Rear wall: two hieratic graffiti with cartouches of Ramesses II.

43. S. wall: Viceroy Messuy before Re-Harakhti.

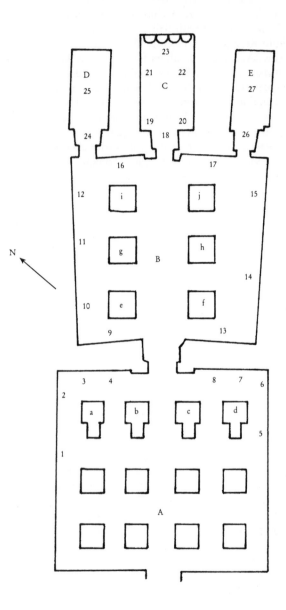

6: The Temple of Derr

A. First pillared hall.
B. Second pillared hall.
C. Sanctuary.
D. Side-chamber with shelf.
E. Side-chamber.

. Much destroyed: Ramesses II in chariot.
2. 1st row: king offers wine to Atum; 2nd row: king offers prisoners
to Re-Harakhti.
. King with *ka* and lion smiting enemies before Re-Harakhti.
. 1st row: king, two gods; 2nd row: king offers Maat to Khnum.
–4. Below, 8 princes.
. Fleeing Nubians.
. 1st row: king offers vases to Onuris; 2nd row: king offers prisoners
to Amun-Re.
. King with *ka* and lion smiting enemies before Amun-Re.
. 1st row: king offers wine to Ptah; 2nd row: king offers incense,
libation to Thoth.
–8. Below, 9 princesses.

Osirid Pillars: inscription beneath statue on east face; two scenes on
other three faces:
. N: king receives life from Horus of Baki; flail from Horus of
Buhen; W: king receives life from Horus of Buhen; offers incense to
Horus; S: king offers incense to Nefertum; wine to Khonsu.
. N: king receives life from Sekhmet; before Mut; W: king receives life
from Montu; offers incense to Isis; S: king before Amun-Re;
receives 'jubilee' symbol from Atum.
. N: king receives life from Nefertum; 'jubilee' symbol from Amun-
Re; W: king offers flowers to Khonsu; wine to Mut; S: king receives
life from Amun-Re; 'jubilee' symbol from Re-Harakhti.
. N: king anoints Ptah; worships Montu; W: king receives life from
Thoth; from Horus of Buhen; S: king receives life from Atum;
from Re-Harakhti.

. King led by Atum, Harsiesi to Re-Harakhti, Iusas.
0. King offers flowers to sacred bark of Re-Harakhti carried by
priests with self as high priest in leopard skin.
1. King offers wine to Amun-Re-Kamutef, Isis.
2. Thoth writes king's name on sacred tree; king receives name from
Ptah, Sekhmet.

13. King receives 'jubilee' symbol from Sefkhet-abu; is purified by Harsiesi, Thoth.

14. King offers incense, libation to sacred bark of Re-Harakhti carried by priests with self as high priest in leopard skin.

15. King with Thoth, Montu, Harsiesi; receives 'jubilee' symbol from Amun-Re, Mut in shrine.

Pillars: Ramesses II with a deity on each face:

e. E: Amun-Re; S: Mut; W: Horus of Miam; N: Ptah.

f. E: Atum; S: Thoth; W: Khnum; N: Re-Harakhti.

g. E: Isis; S: Atum; W: Onuris; N: Amun-Re.

h. E: Menhit; S: Re-Harakhti; W: Khonsu; N: Montu.

i. E: Amun-Re; S: Inyt; W: Montu; N: Re-Harakhti.

j. E: Mut; S: Atum; W: Isis; N: Horus.

16. King offers incense, libation to Re-Harakhti, Hathor.

17. King offers Maat to Amun-Re with deified Ramesses II, Mut.

18. Doorway to sanctuary: lintel, double-scene; l: king runs with *hap* and oar; r: with vases to gods (destroyed); jambs (damaged), l: king before Re-Harakhti, Horus; r: before Horus, Atum. Passage: l: text, king receives life from Amun-Re; r: text, king receives life from Re-Harakhti.

19, 20. King with libation vase.

21. L–r: king offers incense, libation to bark of Re-Harakhti, deified Ramesses II; offers cloth to Ptah.

22. R–l: king offers incense, libation to bark of Re-Harakhti, deified Ramesses II; anoints Re-Harakhti.

23. L–r: statues of Ptah, Amun-Re, deified Ramesses II, Re-Harakhti (all much damaged).

24. Doorway to left (north) side-chapel: above, mummiform figures of Osiris, Harsiesi, Seth, Isis, another deity; lintel, double-scene, king with vases before Re; jambs, royal titles. Passage: l: king with Horus of Baki.

25. Each side of doorway, Ramesses II; left wall, l–r: king offers incense to Atum; cloth to Amun-Re; vases to Re-Harakhti; rear wall, double-scene, king offers vases to Horus; right wall, l–r: king runs with *hap* and oar to deified Ramesses II; offers collar to Mut, incense to Khonsu.

26. Doorway to right (south) side-chapel: above, mummiform figure of Montu, Atum, Shu, Tefnut; lintel, double-scene, king before (Re-Harakhti); jambs, royal titles. Passage: l: king receives life from Horus of Baki.

7. Left of doorway, Ramesses II; l.eft wall, l–r: king offers cakes to Ptah; incense to Amun-Re; bread to Re-Harakhti; rear wall, double-scene, king offers to deified Ramesses II; right wall, l–r: king offers incense, libation to Re-Harakhti; runs with vases to Osiris, Isis, Harsiesi.

7: The Tomb of Pennut

, Pennut and wife Takha.

1st row: Pennut and doorway; Pennut and wife before Thoth; 'Declaration of Innocence' text; 2nd row: l: mourning women; rest destroyed; top of balance from Weighing of the Heart scene just visible at right.

1st row: l: Horus leads Pennut and wife to Osiris, Isis, Nephthys; r: inscription (damaged); 2nd row: destroyed.

1st row: l: Pennut worships Hathor-cow in Western Mountain; with hippo-goddess, pyramid-tomb; r: Pennut and wife before Re-Khepri; 2nd row: l: Pennut purified by Anubis, Thoth before Re-Harakhti; r: Pennut and wife before (Ptah-Sokar-Osiris).

1st row: Endowment inscription for Ramesses VI statue (damaged); 2nd row: l: two women from offering scene on adjacent wall; (rest destroyed).

1st row: r: Pennut attired by servants; (rest of wall to left destroyed); 2nd row: r: relatives; (rest of wall to left destroyed).

1st row: Pennut and wife with six sons before Re-Harakhti; 2nd row: l: Pennut and wife (legs only) before Osiris; (rest of wall to right destroyed).

Doorway to niche: lintel, baboons adoring bark of Re with sun-disk; niche: three unfinished statues, middle one cow-headed.

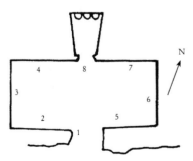

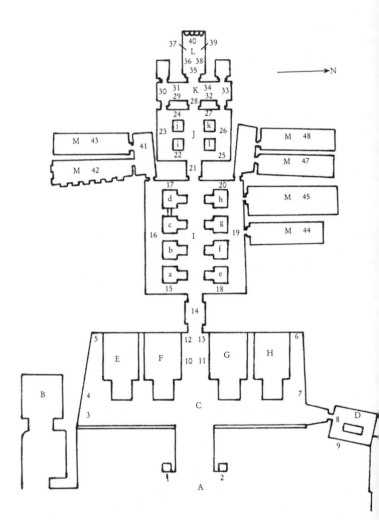

8: The Great Temple, Abu Simbel

A. Forecourt.
B. Chapel of Thoth.
C. Terrace.
D. Chapel of Re-Harakhti;
   altar in center.
E–H. Colossi of Ramesses II.

I. Great pillared hall.
J. Second pillared hall.
K. Vestibule.
L. Sanctuary.
M. Storerooms.

1. Stela: Ramesses II offers incense to Amen-Re, Ptah, Isis.
2. Stela: Ramesses II offers flowers to Amen-Re, Re-Harakhti, Thoth.
3. Stela: Hittite Marriage, Ramesses II receives the princess and her father, Hattusil III.
4. Stela: Ambassador Rekhpehtuf, reign of Siptah; reappointment of Sety as viceroy.
5. Stela: Ramesses II offers wine to Amun-Re, Re-Harakhti, Horus-Ha.
6. Stela: double-scene, Ramesses II offers wine to Re-Harakhti.
7. Stela: Siptah before Amun-Re, Mut, Re-Harakhti, Seth, Astarte; below, viceroy Sety with son and grandson.
8. King with Amun-Re, Re-Harakhti, Ptah, Atum, Thoth, Isis, Min-Amun.
9. False pylon, king before Re-Harakhti, Amun-Re.
10. Nubian prisoners.
11. Asiatic and Libyan prisoners.
12, 13. *Sma-tawi* motif, Nile-gods tying lotus and papyrus.
14. Entrance doorway: lintel, Ramesses II runs (left) with *hap* and oar to Amun-Re, Mut; (right) with vases to Re-Harakhti, Isis. Passage: king and royal titles. Inner side: lintel, king before Re-Harakhti and Sekhmet, Amun-Re and Mut. Jambs: king offers (left) to Min, Khonsu, Atum; (right) to Amun-Re, Ptah, Re-Harakhti.
15. King with *ka* smites Nubian and Hittite prisoners before Amun-Re; 8 princes below.
16. 1st row: l–r, king offers incense and libation to ram-headed Merymutef and lioness goddess Ipt, boxes of cloth to Amun-Re, incense to Ptah; king with Thoth and Seshat writing; king kneels under sacred tree before Re-Harakhti, Thoth writes names on leaves; king before uraeus and Amun-Re (representing Amun in the sacred mountain of Gebel Barkal); 2nd row: l–r, Nubian, Syrian, Libyan wars; king with sons in chariots attacks Syrian fortress; herdsman and cattle; king smiting and trampling on Libyans; king in his chariot with lion and Nubian prisoners.

17. King presents Nubian prisoners to Amun-Re, deified Ramesses II, Mut.
18. King with *ka* smites Libyan prisoners before Re-Harakhti; 9 princesses below; left end, under princesses, graffiti of sculptor Piay and offering-bearer Panufer, (written vertically).
19. Battle of Kadesh: l–r, recruits arriving with chariots; Egyptian camp; town of Kadesh and battle; king in chariot; Egyptian and enemy chariots; battle record of Year 5; king on throne, courtiers, officers, pile of hands; arrival of division of Ptah. Underneath, graffiti of priests' names.
20. King presents Hittite prisoners to Re-Harakhti, deified Ramesses II, Iusas.

Osirid pillars (2 registers on each side):
a. E: king offers to Ramesses II, queen offers to Hathor of Abshek; S: king offers to Raettawi, Termuthis; W: king offers to Min, Isis.
b. E: king offers to Amun-Re, Ptah; S: king offers to Sobek-Re, Amun-Re; W: king offers to Merymutef, ram-headed Montu.
c. E: king before Isis, Hathor; S: king offers to Wert-Hekau, Princess Bint-Anath offers to Anukis; W: king offers to Thoth, king faces Horus of Buhen.
Between pillars c and d is the 'Blessing of Ptah' Stela.
d. E: king offers to Re-Harakhti, king faces Amun-Re; S: king offers to Sheps of Hermopolis, Osiris; W: king offers to Onuris-Shu, Amun-Re of Karnak.
e. E: king offers to Menhit, Onuris-Shu; N: king offers to Khnum, Anukis; W: king offers to Thoth, Satis.
f. E: king offers to Horus of Baki, Mut; N: king offers to Re, Hathor; W: king offers to Anukis, Horus of Miam.
g. E: king offers to Thoth, Atum; N: king offers to Amun-Re, Horus-Ha; W: king offers to Anubis, Khnum.
h. E: king offers to Amun-Re, Re-Harakhti; N: king offers to Re, Hathor; W: king offers to crocodile-headed Amun, Min-Amun-Kamutef, Isis.

21. Doorway to second hall: above, double-scene, king before sphinx; lintel, l: king runs with *hap* and oar to Amun-Re, Mut, r: king runs with vase and flail to Re-Harakhti, Tefnut; jambs, l: king offers to Min, Atum, r: to Ptah, Montu; passage, l: king offers flowers to Re, r: offers incense to Amun.
22. King offers flowers to Amun-Re, deified Ramesses II (later addition), Mut.

23. King and Queen Nefertari offer to bark of Amun-Re carried by priests.

24. King before Amun-Re.

25. King offers lettuces to Min-Amun, deified Ramesses II (inserted later), and Isis.

26. King and queen before bark of deified Ramesses II carried by priests.

27. King receives jubilee from Re-Harakhti.

Pillars in second pillared hall:

. E: king (falcon-headed) with Anubis; S: with Satis; W: with Wert-Hekau; N: with Horus of Miam.

. E: king with Mut; S: with Wadjet; W: with Horus of Maha; N: with Amun-Re.

. E: destroyed; S: king with Hathor; W: with Horus of Baki; N: with Horus of Buhen.

. E: king with Mut; S: with Ramesses II; W: with Montu; N: with Hathor.

28. Doorways to vestibule: passage, king before Ramesses II; north doorway, passage, l: king receives life from Amun-Re; r: receives life from deified Ramesses II.

29. King offers wine to Min-Amun-Kamutef.

30. King offers wine to Horus-Ha.

31. King offers incense to ram-headed Amun-Re.

32. King offers bread to Atum.

33. King offers Maat to Thoth.

34. King offers flowers to Ptah in shrine.

35. Doorway to sanctuary: above, double-scene, king offers to Amun-Re and Mut, to deified Ramesses and Maat; jambs, l: king before Ramesses II, Osiris, r: before Ramesses, Ptah.

36. Ramesses II.

37. King before bark of Amun-Re, anoints Min-Amun-Kamutef.

38. Ramesses II.

39. King before bark of deified Ramesses II and before deified self.

40. Four seated statues, l–r: Ptah, Amun-Re, Ramesses II, Re-Harakhti.

Storerooms:

41. South side, l–r: king offers to ram-headed Amun-Re; king; king before Horus; king between Amun-Re and Atum; before Re, Thoth; king offers to Ptah, Min-Amun, Isis, Ramesses II.

42. L–r: dedication inscription above niches; king offers to Ptah, Montu, Thoth, Amun-Ra; before Amun, Kamutef, Re-Harakhti.

43. L–r: king offers to Re, Amun-Re, Isis, Atum, Thoth; double-
    scene, king offers to Re, Ramesses II; offers to Re, Sheps, Re-
    Harakhti, Thoth, Horus of Miam, ram-headed Amun-Re.
44. Left side only decorated: large cartouche; king offers to ram-headed
    Amun-Re, Re-Harakhti, Ramesses II, Horus of Buhen, Horus of
    Miam, Horus of Baki.
45. L–r: king before Isis, offers to Re-Harakhti, ram-headed Amun-
    Re, Ptah, Khonsu, Ramesses II (twice), Thoth; double-scene, king
    offers Maat and incense to Amun-Re; offers to Thoth, Sheps of
    Hermopolis, Atum, Horus of Buhen, Horus of Baki, Horus of
    Miam, Re; Hathor seated.
46. L–r: king with *ka* offers to Amun-Re Kamutef, Isis; Amun with
    Mut and Khonsu; Atum; double-scene, king offers wine to Re, ram-
    headed Amun-Re; offers to Ramesses II; receives life from Ramesses
    II; before Montu; offers to Thoth.
47. L–r: king before Amun-Re; offers to Wepwawet, Khonsu, Khepri;
    drives 4 calves to Khnum; Isis before offering-stand; double-scene,
    king offers to Re; Thoth seated; king before Re; offers to Isis,
    Montu, Thoth, Ptah, another god.
48. L–r: king offers to Ramesses II; to Re, Ptah, Sekhmet, Anubis;
    before Ramesses II; double-scene, offers wine to Re, ram-headed
    Amun-Re; king's cartouches with Thoth; king offers to Isis, Amun-
    Re, Ramesses II, Montu.

9: The Small Temple, Abu Simbel

A, C, D, F. Ramesses II statues.

B, E. Nefertari statues.

G. Pillared hall.

H. Vestibule.

I. Sanctuary.

1. Entrance. Lintel, double-scene, l: king offers wine to Amun-Re; r: incense to Horus-Ha; jambs, royal titles; passage, l: royal titles, king offers flowers to Hathor of Abshek, royal titles; r: royal titles, queen offers flowers to Isis, royal titles.

2. Ramesses II (with Nefertari behind) smites Nubian prisoner before Amun-Re.

3. King receives *menit*-necklace from Hathor.

4. King crowned by Horus of Maha and Seth of Nubet.

5. Queen offers sistrum and flowers to Anukis.

6. King offers Maat to Amun-Re.

7. Queen with flowers and sistrum before Hathor of Abshek.

8. Ramesses II (with *ka* and Nefertari behind) smites Asiatic prisoner before Horus of Maha.

9. King presents offerings to Ptah in shrine.

10. King offers flowers to ram-headed Harsaphes.

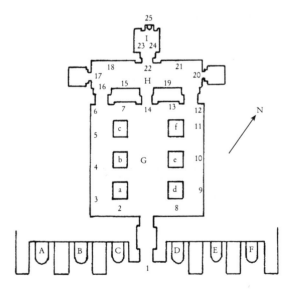

11. Queen before Hathor of Dendera.
12. King offers wine to Re-Harakhti.
13. Queen offers flowers to Mut.

Hathor pillars:
Offering inscription and royal titles on aisle face.
South row:
a. E: queen with sistrum, papyrus; S: queen with sistrum; W: Horus of Buhen.
b. E: Thoth; S: Maat; W: Satis.
c. E: queen with flowers; S: Hathor; W: Isis.
North row:
d. E: queen with sistrum; N: king offers flowers; W: Horus of Miam.
e. E: king with incense; N: Mut of Asher (Karnak); W: Horus of Baki
f. E: Khnum; N: Khonsu; W: Isis.

14. Entrances to vestibule. Middle doorway, lintel, royal titles; jambs, Ramesses II. Side doorways, lintels and jambs, royal titles.
15. Queen crowned by Hathor of Abshek, Isis.
16. Over doorway, queen's name between two vultures.
17. Over doorway, queen offers flowers to Hathor-cow on boat.
18. King offers flowers to Horuses of Miam, Baki, Buhen, wine to Amun-Re.
19. King and queen offer flowers to Taweret.
20. Over doorway, king offers flowers to Hathor-cow in boat.
21. King offers wine to Re-Harakhti, queen offers flowers to Khnum, Satis, Anukis.
22. Doorway to sanctuary. Outer lintel, king and queen before Hathor, Mut; jambs, Ramesses II. Inner lintel, Nile-god on each side, queen's titles above.
23. Queen with incense and sistrum before Mut, Hathor.
24. King with incense and libation before deified Ramesses II, Queen Nefertari.
25. Niche, statue of Hathor-cow, king under chin, between two Hathor pillars; l: king offering flowers.

Chronology

Nubia	Egypt
c. *12000* BC Semi-nomadic hunter–gatherers	Semi-nomadic hunter–gatherers in southern Upper Egypt
c. *6000* BC Khartoum Mesolithic Culture	c. *5000* BC Badarian Culture
c. *4000* Earliest settlements in Lower Nubia	*4000–3600* Naqada I
c. *3500* Development of A-Group Culture	*3600–3200* Naqada II
	3300–3100 Naqada III
	3100 Unification of Upper & Lower Egypt
	3100–2696 Archaic Period: Dynasties 1 & 2
2278–2184 Harkhuf's expeditions	*2696–2184* Old Kingdom: Dynasties 3–6
c. *2200* Dispersal of A-Group Culture	
2200–1570 C-Group Culture in Lower Nubia	*2184–2040* 1st Intermediate Period: Dynasties 7–10
	2040–1782 Middle Kingdom: Dynasties 11 & 12
1990–1570 Kerma Culture in Upper Nubia	*1971–1926* Senusert I
	1878–1841 Senusert III

Nubia	Egypt
	1782–1570 2nd Intermediate Period: Dynasties 13–17 (Dynasties 15 & 16 Hyksos)
1570–1070 Nubia a province of Egypt	*1570–1070* New Kingdom: Dynasties 18, 19 & 20
1527 Destruction of Kerma by Tuthmosis I	*1524–1518* Tuthmosis I
1475 Tuthmosis III founds Napata, Upper Nubia; Temples of Amada & al-Lesiya built, & shrines at Qasr Ibrim	*1504–1450* Tuthmosis III
c. *1446* Amenophis II completes Amada Temple; Viceroy Usersatet makes shrine at Ibrim	*1453–1419* Amenophis II
c. *1415* Tuthmosis IV adds to Amada Temple	*1419–1386* Tuthmosis IV
c. *1360* Amenophis III builds temples of Soleb & Sedeinga to deified self & Queen Tiye in Upper Nubia	*1386–1349* Amenophis III
c. *1255* Temples at Abu Simbel dedicated	*1279–1212* Ramesses II
1244–29 Temples of Derr, Wadi al-Sebua, Gerf Hussein, & Beit al-Wali built	
	1069–525 3rd Int. Period: Dynasties 21–26
760–593 The Napatan Period	

Nubia	Egypt
760 Kashta king at Napata	760 Kashta invades Upper Egypt
747–656 Piye founds Egyptian 25th Dynasty	747–656 Dynasty 25 (Kushite)
	674 Assyrian invasion under Esarhaddon: Taharka flees to Thebes
	667–666 Taharka defeated by Assyrians under Ashurbanipal; flees to Nubia
	664 Thebes sacked
	664–525 Dynasty 26
	595–589 Psammetichus II
593 Psammetichus II attacks Nubia; Capital moved to Meroe	
593 BC – AD 350 Meroitic Period	525–332 Late Period: Dynasties 27–30
	525–404 First Persian Period: Dynasty 27
	404–343 Dynasties 28–30 (Egyptian)
	332 Invasion of Alexander the Great
	332–30 Ptolemaic Period
00 BC Burials moved from Napata to Meroe	
Arkamani of Meroe	222–205 Ptolemy IV
	30 BC Death of Cleopatra VII
	30 BC – AD 395 Roman Period
3 BC Queen Amanirenas' attack on Aswan	
1 BC Roman frontier set at Maharraqa	

Nubia	Egypt
	AD *43* Christianity comes to Egypt
	394 Theodosius I makes Christianity state religion
	395–640 Byzantine Period
AD *450* Blemmyes & Nobatae attack Philae	
453 Agreement between Romans & Blemmyes	
535 Philae closed under Justinian	
5th & 6th centuries: Ballana Culture	
543 Christianity comes to Kingdom of Nobatia	
569 Kingdoms of Makuria & Alwa convert to Christianity	
	640 Arab conquest of Egypt
652 Treaty between Christian Nubia & Muslim Egypt	*640–1250* Arab rulers
700 Kingdoms of Nobatia & Makuria unite	
1173 Attack on Qasr Ibrim by Turanshah	
	1250–1517 Mamluks
1315 Christian king Kerenbes replaced by Muslim ruler	
	1517–1882 Ottoman Period
16th century: Fung conquest of Alwa & Lower Nubia	
	1798–1801 French occupation
	1805–1882 Muhammad Ali & his descendants

Nubia	Egypt
1820–1825 Egyptian annexation of Nubia	
	1869 Opening of Suez Canal
	1882–1922 British Protectorate
	1896 General Kitchener recovers Sudan with Egyptian forces
	1899 Anglo-Egyptian Condominium in Sudan
1902 Aswan Dam completed	
1912 Aswan Dam raised	
1934 Aswan Dam raised for last time	
	1952 Egyptian Revolution
1954 Decision to build High Dam at Aswan	
	1956 Sudan becomes independent
	1956 Suez Crisis
1960 Work starts on High Dam	
1960–80 UNESCO Nubian Rescue Campaign	
1964 Last Nubians evacuated	
1970 High Dam completed	

Gods and Goddesses
on the Nubian Monuments

Amaunet: Goddess whose name means 'the hidden one.' Consort of Amun, largely superceded by Mut from the New Kingdom onward.

Amun: 'The hidden one,' fertility and creator god of ancient Thebes, depicted in the form of a man with a headdress of two tall plumes.

Amun-Re: New Kingdom combination of Amun with the sun god Re and known as the 'king of the gods.'

Amun-Re-Kamutef: 'Amun-Re, bull of his mother,' ithyphallic form of Amun-Re closely associated with the fertility god Min.

Anukis: Goddess of the cataract area at Aswan and third member of the triad of Elephantine with Khnum and Satis. Sometimes regarded as consort and sometimes as daughter of Khnum. Shown as a woman with a crested headdress.

Arsaphes: Egyptian *Heryshef*, 'he who is upon his lake.' Ram-god of fertility worshiped at Herakleopolis near modern Beni Suef.

Arsenuphis: Meroitic god, perhaps of Egyptian origin, his name meaning 'the good companion.' Warrior god associated with Shu.

Astarte: Warrior-goddess of Canaan and Syria absorbed into the Egyptian pantheon in the Eighteenth Dynasty as daughter of Re and wife of Seth.

Atum: Ancient creator god associated with the sun cult. Depicted as a man wearing the double crown, or the *nemes* headcloth, sometimes leaning on a staff.

Dedwen: Nubian god, bringer of incense, believed to burn incense at royal births.

Geb: Earth-god, son of Shu and Tefnut and brother-husband of the sky-goddess Nut. The children of Geb and Nut were Osiris, Isis, Seth, and Nephthys.

Harpocrates: Egyptian *Har-pa-khered*, 'Horus the Child.' Divine child, son of Isis and Osiris, manifested as a vulnerable child.

Harsiesi: 'Horus, son of Isis,' an aspect of Horus as heir of his father, Osiris.

Hathor: Cow-goddess of love, beauty, and music. As goddess of the West she personifies the way to the afterlife. Shown as a woman with a crown of cow's horns and sun-disk, as she was a daughter of Re.

Horus: Falcon god of kingship, sky god, and solar deity. In the legend of Osiris, the son of Isis and Osiris. Worshiped in Nubia in forms associated with various localities: Horus of Miam (Aniba), Horus of Baki (Quban), Horus of Maha (Abu Simbel), and Horus of Buhen. Depicted with a man's body and a falcon's head, usually wearing the double crown.

Horus-Ha: Horus associated with Ha, Lord of the West, a protector god of the Western Desert.

Inyt: Goddess of Armant and consort of Montu.

Ipt: Goddess of the town of Khait, between Asyut and Qusiya. Consort of Merymutef.

Isis: Great mother goddess, sister and wife of Osiris, mother of Horus, and mistress of magic.

Iusas: Personification of the female principle in creation.

Khepri: Creator god of the rising sun in the form of the scarab beetle.

Khnum: Ram-headed god, worshiped at Aswan as lord of Elephantine, guardian of the cataract and the inundation, with his consorts Satis and Anukis. At Esna, with the lioness goddess Menhit as his consort, Khnum is worshiped as a creator god who fashioned people on his potter's wheel.

Khonsu: Moon god, son of Amun-Re and Mut of Karnak. Sometimes depicted as a child with sidelock, sometimes as a falcon-headed man with the full and crescent moons on his head.

Maat: Goddess of truth and justice. Shown as a woman with a feather on her head. The king often presented a figure of Maat to the gods.

Mandulis: Egyptian *Merwel*, a god of Lower Nubia associated with Egyptian Horus as a solar deity. Shown as a man with a crown of ram's horns, plumes, sun-disks, and cobras. Depicted also in his temple at Kalabsha with a falcon's body and a man's head with characteristic headdress.

Menhit: Lioness-headed consort of Khnum at Esna.

Merymutef: Ram god of the town of Khait between Asyut and Qusiya. Perhaps a local form of Khnum.

Miket: Goddess of the First Cataract region associated with the Elephantine triad of Khnum, Satis, and Anukis.

Min: Fertility god and guardian of desert and mining areas east of the Nile. Shown in ithyphallic form with one arm upraised, often with cos lettuces on a table behind him. In the New Kingdom he is occasionally combined with the sun god as Min-Re.

Montu: God of war originating in the Theban area. Falcon-headed with a crown of two plumes and the sun-disk. In the New Kingdom he is associated with the king's conquest of foreign lands.

Mut: Consort of Amun of Thebes, sometimes associated with Sekhmet as a lioness. Shown as a woman wearing a vulture headdress surmounted by a double crown.

Nebethetepet: Goddess of Heliopolis, a form of Hathor as the female creative principle.

Nefertum: Memphite god of the blue lotus flower from which the sun rose, son of Ptah and Sekhmet. Shown as a man with lotus flower headdress.

Nehemawat: Rarely mentioned goddess, consort of Thoth of Hermopolis.

Nekhbet: Vulture goddess of Upper Egypt, corresponding to Wadjet, cobra goddess of Lower Egypt. Shown as a vulture over the king's head or a woman in the white crown of Upper Egypt.

Nephthys: Sister of Osiris, Isis, and Seth, who was also her consort. From a liaison with Osiris, she was the mother of Anubis. With her sister Isis, closely connected with funerary beliefs through the Osiris legend.

Nut: Sky-goddess, daughter of Shu and Tefnut, sister-wife of the earth-god Geb.Believed to swallow the sun-god each evening and give birth to him each morning, so associated with beliefs of resurrection and rebirth.

Onuris-Shu: Warrior god of war and hunting, depicted as a bearded man wearing a headdress of tall plumes. Associated with Shu; has a similar legend of bringing his consort back from Nubia.

Osiris: Judge of the dead and lord of eternity. Brother and husband of Isis, father of Horus. The legend of his murder by his brother Seth and his subsequent resurrection made him the principal god of the afterlife. Usually depicted mummiform with a crown of ram's horns surmounted by the white crown with a feather on each side.

Ptah: Creator god, patron of artisans, and god of ancient Memphis. Depicted mummiform wearing a blue skull-cap, often in a shrine. His consort was the lioness-headed goddess Sekhmet.

Ptah-Nun: Combination of Path and Nun, the personification of the primeval ocean, as the father of the creator-god Atum.

Ptah-Tatenen: Earth god of Memphis, personification of the primeval mound, the first piece of land at the beginning of creation.

Raettawi: Solar goddess, consort of Montu.

Re: Principal sun god, creator god of Heliopolis. Shown as a falcon-headed man with the sun-disk surrounded by a cobra on his head. In the underworld in the form of a ram. Often combined with other gods to increase their power.

Re-Harakhti: Combined form of Re and Horus of the Horizon. Depicted falcon-headed with the sun-disk.

atis: Goddess of the cataract and the Nile flood. Consort of Khnum of Elephantine. Also goddess of fertility, worshiped throughout Nubia. Depicted as a woman in a white crown with horns.

efkhet-abu: New Kingdom form of Seshat, goddess of writing and record-keeping. Particularly associated with the foundation ceremony and writing the king's name on the sacred tree. Shown as a woman wearing a leopard-skin and a curious headdress of a star on a long pole with reversed horns above.

ekhmet: Lioness-goddess, consort of Ptah of Memphis. 'Eye of Re' as instrument of punishment, bringing death and destruction. Also regarded as a goddess of medicine, in the belief that she could cure disease as well as inflict it.

erapis: Hybrid god with aspects of Osiris and the Greek god Zeus, introduced into Egypt by Ptolemy I. Represented as a bearded man with a grain measure on his head.

eth: First found as patron god of Nubet (modern Naqada), north of Luxor. God of the deserts and foreign lands, champion of the sun god and protector of the king. Later god of evil through his role in the Osiris legend.

heps: 'The noble one,' god of Hermopolis, associated with the heavens, the sun, the moon, and the stars.

hu: God of air, son of Atum, and brother of Tefnut. Shown as a man with a feather on his head.

obek-Re: The crocodile-god combined with the sun-god Re. As a god of watery places, Sobek was worshiped at difficult stretches of the Nile, such as the cataracts.

okar: Falcon-headed god of the Memphite cemetery at Saqqara, closely associated with Ptah and later also Osiris.

aweret: Hippopotamus goddess, protector of women in childbirth.

efnut: Lioness goddess of moisture, sister and consort of Shu, and 'eye of Re.' Legend of her rampage in Nubia, until persuaded by Shu and Thoth to return to Egypt.

ermouthis: Harvest goddess Renenutet, in Greco-Roman Period identified with Isis as mother goddess.

Thenent (or Tjenenet): Consort of Montu in the Theban area. A goddess of childbirth, who attended the birth of a king and was also associated with the symbolic rebirth of the soul in the afterlife.

Thoth: Lunar god of knowledge, inventor of writing, messenger of the gods. Manifested as baboon or ibis; usually depicted as an ibis-headed man. Cult center at Hermopolis in Middle Egypt. Worshiped in the Nubian Temple of Dakka in his local form, Thoth of Pnubs (the sycamore fig tree), where he is shown as a man with a plumed headdress on top of a short, Nubian wig.

Tutu: Roman Period protector god, a combination of sphinx and griffin. Son of creator goddess Neith of Sais in the western Delta. Also worshiped in the Roman town of Kellis, Dakhla Oasis, Western Desert. The feast of Neith and Tutu was celebrated at Esna.

Wadjet: Cobra goddess of Lower Egypt, counterpart of Nekhbet, vulture goddess of Upper Egypt. Lioness aspect a 'eye of Re,' and as nurse of the infant Horus, later identified with Isis. Appears in the Temple of Kalabsha as the partner of Mandulis, the Nubian form of Horus as solar deity.

Wepset: 'She who burns,' one of the names of the fire-spitting cobra (uraeus) and the goddess as the Eye of Re who was brought back from Nubia. At Philae and other Greco-Roman temples in Nubia, such as Dakka, she is equated with Tefnut.

Wepwawet: Jackal-god of Upper Egypt, whose name means 'opener of the ways.' Associated with pharaoh's military prowess, as well as opening the way to the Underworld.

Wert-Hekau: 'Great of magic,' the royal uraeus as a cobra goddess. Usually shown either cobra- or lion-headed although on an Abu Simbel pillar (i; west side) in human form. Another manifestation of the solar eye, who protected the sun god. Title of the goddesses Mut and Isis.

Glossary

abacus (pl. abaci): Square block of stone at the top of a column between the capital and the architrave.

Abydos: Burial place of the First Dynasty kings and later cult center of Osiris, god of the dead.

ambulatory: Corridor around the rear part of a temple, usually roofless; a feature of Greco-Roman temples.

ankh: Hieroglyphic sign for 'life' in the form of a looped cross, probably representing a sandal thong.

apse: Semi-circular portion forming the sanctuary area of a Christian church.

architrave: Horizontal beam across the tops of columns.

atef-crown: Elaborate headdress with ram's horns, cobras, plumes, and sun-disks; a development of the crown of Osiris.

Ayyubid: Pertaining to the dynasty of descendants of the Kurdish ruler Ayyub, who ruled Egypt in the twelfth century AD.

baboon: Ape sacred to Thoth, god of wisdom; also sacred to the sun god as worshiper of the rising sun, inspired by the antics of real baboons at sunrise.

baptistry: Part of the church where infants and converts are baptized.

capital: Top part of the column shaft, usually carved in plant form.

cartouche: Oval ring in which the king's personal and throne names are written; derived from the hieroglyphic symbol *shen*, a coil of rope, meaning 'all that the sun encircles.'

cataract: Rock formations cutting across the river bed and breaking up the natural flow.

Chief Wife: Most important of the king's wives, through whom succession to the throne passed on to the children.

cobra: Hooded snake, manifestation of Wadjet, patron goddess of Lower Egypt; also royal uraeus on the forehead of the king for protection.

colossus (pl. colossi): Larger than life-size, colossal statue.

composite capital: Greco-Roman style of top of column with a complex design combining different, sometimes imaginary, floral forms.

Coptic: Egyptian Christian people, language, and art; derived via Arabic from Greek name for Egypt, *Aegyptos*.

cosmetic palette: Small stone palette used for grinding and mixing make-up, such as malachite or galena (lead sulfide) for eye shadow.

crypt: Underground chambers in a temple or church; used in a temple for storing valuable items.

dado: Horizontal band of decoration at the bottom of a wall.

demotic: Extremely cursive Egyptian script derived from hieroglyphs; developed around 700 BC and used until about AD 450, especially for everyday documents.

diorite: Hard black stone with large white flecks, used for statues.

Dodekaschoinos: The 'twelve *schoinos* strip' in Lower Nubia between Philae and Maharraqa, regarded as the Estate of Isis in the Greco-Roman Period; a *schoinos* is about ten kilometers.

doum-palm: Type of palm tree with divided trunk, which produces the large doum nut that can be chewed.

double crown: Combination of the red crown of Lower Egypt and the white crown of Upper Egypt, worn by deities as well as the pharaoh.

EAO: Egyptian Antiquities Organization, now the Supreme Council for Antiquities (SCA); government body responsible for antiquities, ancient monuments, and museums.

Edfu: Cult center of the falcon god of kingship, Horus of Behdet, in Upper Egypt, about one hundred kilometers south of Luxor.

faience: Glazed composition, usually quartz, molded in different colors, especially blue/green; used for jewelry, statuettes, tiles, small vessels.

false beard: Ceremonial beard worn by the pharaoh as a symbol of authority; attached to the edge of the crown by tapes.

foundation ceremony: Series of rituals connected with the founding and dedication of a temple, including running 'a ritual course' and 'stretching the cord.'

Fung Dynasty: People of unknown origin from southeast Sudan, who established their capital at Sennar on the Blue Nile in the early sixteenth century and dominated the region as far as the Third Cataract for the next three hundred years.

God's Wife of Amun: Administrative and priestly title at Thebes held by princesses of the New Kingdom and Twenty-fifth and Twenty-sixth Dynasties.

hap: V-shaped instrument connected with navigation, perhaps part of the steering gear; often held by the king when running a 'ritual course,' with an oar in his other hand.

heb-sed: King's jubilee festival, usually celebrated in the thirtieth year of his reign.

hemi-speos: Temple or shrine which is half, or partly, rock-cut.

hieroglyphs: 'Sacred writing,' detailed picture-writing of the ancient Egyptians, in use from about 3200 BC; used increasingly for religious purposes only with the development of the cursive script, hieratic, from about 2700 BC onward.

Hittites: People of Anatolia, eastern Turkey, who threatened Egyptian influence in Syria in the New Kingdom.

Hyksos: Semitic people from Western Asia of mixed origins, who gradually settled in the Delta in the late Middle Kingdom, and formed the Fifteenth and Sixteenth Dynasties.

hypostyle hall: Pillared hall in Egyptian temples symbolizing marsh plants on the primeval mound.

ibis: Wading bird of the heron family; the sacred ibis (white with a long curved bill and black head and tail) was a manifestation of Thoth, god of wisdom and learning, but is no longer seen in Egypt.

Imhotep: Chief minister of Zoser of the Third Dynasty and traditionally believed to be the architect of the Step Pyramid at Saqqara. Worshiped in the Greco-Roman Period as a god of wisdom and medicine.

iunmutef **priest**: The title means 'pillar of his mother'; same as a *sem* priest (see below).

jamb: Side post of a door or window.

jubilee-symbol: Hieroglyphic sign for *heb-sed*, or jubilee festival, consisting of a double shrine with a throne in each side.

ka: Spiritual double, represented by the symbol of two raised arms.

Kandake: Meroitic word for 'queen.'

Karnak: Site of the Temple of Amun-Re at Thebes (Luxor) largest ancient temple ever built.

kiosk: Small shrine of columns and screen-walls, sometimes roofless.

Kom Ombo: Cult center of the crocodile god Sobek, forty kilometers north of Aswan.

libation: Liquid offering, often poured over solid offerings, or into a bowl.

lintel: Horizontal crosspiece over a door or window.

lotus: Water lily, emblem of Upper Egypt.

Mahdi: Means 'rightly guided'; messianic title claimed by charismatic Muslim leader in Sudan, who in 1881 instigated a strongly supported revolt against foreign rule by Egypt and European administrators.

Mamluks: Mercenaries from Turkey and Circassia, on the Black Sea, imported into Egypt as boy-slaves, but later forming a ruling class, AD 1250–1517, and remaining powerful until the early nineteenth century.

Memphis: First capital and primary administrative center of Egypt, founded about 3000 BC and originally called 'White Walls.' 'Memphis' is the Greek version of *Men-nefer*, the name of the pyramid complex of the Sixth Dynasty king Pepi I.

menit-necklace: Thick necklace with multiple strands of beads and a large counterpoise (often decorated with the figure of Hathor). Symbol of Hathor held in the hand by her priestesses.

mortuary temple: Temple for the worship of the king after his death.

naos: Greek word for the sanctuary of a temple, or the shrine within it containing the statue of the god.

nave: Main central aisle of a church.

nemes: Pharaoh's striped headcloth of blue and yellow linen.

Nilometer: Gauge for measuring the rise of the Nile flood, usually consisting of circular or square well with steps marked with a scale.

nomes: Greek term for administrative districts of ancient Egypt, each ruled by a governor or 'nomarch'; in the New Kingdom there were twenty in Lower Egypt and twenty-two in Upper Egypt.

ocher: Red or yellow earthy clay used as a pigment in paints.

Ombos: Greek name for ancient Egyptian Nubet, modern Tukh, near the predynastic site of Naqada, thirty kilometers north of Luxor. The ancient town of Nubet was sacred to the god Seth.

Osirid pillar: Square pillar fronted by a colossal statue of the king as Osiris, with his feet together and hands crossed on his chest holding crook and flail scepters. The king is sometimes shown mummiform like Osiris, sometimes wearing a short kilt (see the great hall of the Great Temple at Abu Simbel, and the open court of the Temple of Wadi al-Sebua).

pantheon: The entire group of gods.

papyrus: Water plant of the sedge family, which grew abundantly in the Nile Delta in ancient times and from which Egyptians made paper. Plant emblem of Lower Egypt.

petroglyphs: Prehistoric rock carvings.

Philae: Island on which the Temple of Isis at Aswan originally stood. The temple was moved to the neighboring island of Agilka after the High Dam was built, but is still referred to by its old location.

podium: Terrace or platform.

primeval mound: First piece of land that emerged from the waters of chaos at the beginning of time; symbol of the act of creation.

pronaos: Forepart of a temple preceding the naos, or sanctuary.

proto-Doric: Type of Egyptian fluted column similar to the Greek Doric column, but predating it by about one thousand years.

pylon: Monumental entrance of an Egyptian temple, consisting of two towers with sloping sides, a doorway in the middle.

rebus: Syllabic depiction of a name.

register: Term used for a line, or row, of carved or painted decoration in Egyptian art.

relief: Carved wall decoration, either raised or sunk. Raised relief has the background cut away (usually found inside buildings); sunk relief is cut into the wall surface (usually on exterior walls).

ritual course: Symbolic course representing a specific area, such as a temple area, or the land of Egypt, around which the king ran holding particular objects for particular occasions.

sacred lake: Artificial lake in temple precincts, where priests washed before participating in temple rituals. It seems to have been replaced by ablutions basins in Nubian temples.

sacristy: Robing-room in a church, where the priest puts on and takes off vestments.

sarcophagus (pl. sarcophagi): A stone coffin.

scimitar: Curved sword, symbolizing victory in pharaonic times.

sem **priest**: Priest wearing a leopard-skin who officiated at a funeral in the role of the deceased's eldest son (same as a *iunmutef* priest above; the titles were sometimes joined together as *sem iunmutef*).

herden: May originate from Sardinia; one of the 'Sea Peoples,' displaced persons moving round the Eastern Mediterranean in the fourteenth to twelfth centuries BC. Sherden wear a distinctive horned helmet. Used as mercenaries in the army of Ramesses II.

istrum (pl. sistra): Metal rattle sacred to the goddess Hathor; held by priestesses in religious ceremonies and thought to drive away evil spirits.

na-tawi motif: Means 'uniting the two lands,' referring to the unification of Upper and Lower Egypt, represented by two river gods (sometimes Horus and Seth), tying together lotus and papyrus plants around the hieroglyphic sign for 'unite' (*sma*, the phonetic symbol of windpipe and lungs).

peos: Rock-cut shrine or temple, such as the temples at Abu Simbel.

phinx: Creature with a lion's body and a human head, usually of the king, symbolizing power. Occasionally with animal head in honor of the god of a temple, such as the falcon-headed sphinxes for Horus at Wadi al-Sebua and the ram-headed sphinxes for Amun at Karnak.

ela (pl. stelae): Round-topped stone with inscription.

retching the cord: Using wooden posts and rope to mark out an area of land for a new temple with the help of Seshat (Sefkhet-abu), goddess of reckoning; one of the foundation ceremonies (see above).

ucco: Plaster used for interior or exterior walls, or for decorative molding.

camore fig: tree of the ficus family native to Egypt, which produces edible figs; regarded as sacred to Hathor, but also much used for carpentry.

hebes: Greek name for ancient Luxor, possibly derived from the ancient name for Karnak, *Ta-ipe iswt*, 'Most splendid of places.' The Egyptian name for Thebes was Waset, meaning 'the Scepter.'

throne name: Also called 'prenomen,' the name taken by the king when he acceded to the throne, and written in cartouche.

triad: Holy family of three, usually father, mother, and child worshiped in an Egyptian temple.

tumulus (pl. tumuli): a burial mound.

uraeus: Cobra on the king's forehead, which represented the 'eye of Re' and protected the king.

vizier: Chief administrator after the pharaoh, similar to a prime minister. In the New Kingdom the office was divided into two for Upper and Lower Egypt.

vulture: Manifestation of Nekhbet, patron goddess of Upper Egypt; also sacred to Mut, consort of Amun of Karnak.

weighing of the heart: Part of the beliefs about the judgment of the dead, when the deceased's heart was symbolically weighed against the feather of Truth, to decide worthiness for the afterlife.

winged sun-disk: Motif representing Horus as god of the sky and protector of the sun god Re. Often carved above temple doorways for protection.

Bibliography

W. Y. Adams, *Nubia, Corridor to Africa* (Penguin Books, 1977).

W. Y. Adams, *Qasr Ibrim: The Late Mediaeval Period* (Egypt Exploration Society, London, 1996).

. Baikie, *Egyptian Antiquities in the Nile Valley* (Methuen, London, 1932).

W. V. Davies, ed., *Egypt and Africa* (British Museum Press, London, 1991).

W. B. Emery, *Egypt in Nubia* (Hutchinson, London, 1965).

G. Hart, *A Dictionary of Egyptian Gods and Goddesses* (Routledge & Kegan Paul, London, 1986).

W. Helck, E. Otto, W. Westendorf, eds., *Lexikon der Ägyptologie*, 6 vols. (Wiesbaden, 1975–86).

. W. Hinkel, *Exodus from Nubia* (Berlin, 1977).

. Hochfield, E. Riefstahl, eds., *Africa in Antiquity I: The Essays* (Brooklyn Museum, New York, 1978).

. O'Connor, *Ancient Nubia: Egypt's Rival in Africa* (University Museum, Pennsylvania, 1993).

. Porter, R. Moss, *Topographical Bibliography, VII: Nubia, the Deserts and Outside Egypt*, revised J. Malek (Griffith Institute, Oxford, 1995).

. Save-Soderbergh, *Temples and Tombs of Ancient Nubia* (Thames & Hudson, London, 1987).

. M. Taylor, *Egypt and Nubia* (British Museum Press, London, 1991).

. G. Trigger, *Nubia under the Pharaohs* (Thames & Hudson, London, 1976).

D. A. Welsby, *The Kingdom of Kush* (British Museum Press London, 1996).

D. Wildung, ed., *Sudan: Ancient Kingdoms of the Nil* (Flammarian, Paris, 1997).

Index